Street Photography of New York City

Street Haunting in the Big Apple

Xiomáro

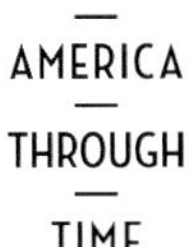

AMERICA
—
THROUGH
—
TIME

AMERICA THROUGH TIME®
An imprint of SUTTON PUBLISHING INC.
www.through-time.com

First published 2025
Copyright © Xiomáro 2025

ISBN 978-1-63499-556-6

Typeset in Gotham Book
Printed and bound in England

Contents

Introduction

The collection of photographs in this book began when I got hit in the face with a tuft of red, white, and blue feathers worn on the head of a woman wearing a G-string, high heels, and body paint.

It happened while I was going home during rush hour one day. Hurrying through the dense crowd, I was lost in thought about catching my train and catching up on my to-do list. Then the spell was suddenly broken.

Floof!

Was it an errant pigeon?

Spitting out fluff, I turned around and was shocked to see that it was a woman and her girlfriend, both practically nude. I had never before heard of or seen these so-called *desnudas* and could not believe they were strolling, unbothered by the police, through a crowd of tourists, families, and businesspeople.

I knew then I had to start photographing my encounters on the street. Not all my experiences were so outlandish. Others were quaint or mundane. They were certainly different from my commissioned work for the National Park Service, and yet still related. With the parks, my photographs often depict "ordinary" life for wealthy white men of European descent, like George Washington, in places restored and staged to recreate historical scenes. On the street, my photographs document diverse people from all walks of life living spontaneously in an unstaged modern urbanscape. Rather than resurrecting the spirits of the dead, I am capturing the spirits of the living.

The epiphany of feathers solved the problem of how to keep my skills sharp in between commissions. I was an attorney at a large midtown law firm. The work hours and the commute from Long Island were both long and unpredictable. It was difficult to schedule outings to go shoot. But photographing on the street provided a daily masterclass as I speed-walked to and from Penn Station and my office. I improved my ability to shoot stealthily, create improvisationally, and frame compositions quickly. In short, I learned how to better use the most important piece of equipment—the one between my ears. My artistic voice became deeper and more expansive.

Discovering Virginia Woolf's mysteriously titled "Street Haunting" gave me a foundation for the aesthetic that was emerging in my images. Woolf's 1927 essay describes the profound impact wandering through London made on her. The fleeting moments and ordinary events of daily life became rich sources of reflection. They sparked imagination about the complex nature of human existence. For Woolf, "to escape is the greatest of pleasures; street haunting ... the greatest of adventures." And so it is for me.

1

The City is an Unread Library

Packed into Manhattan's 23 square miles are millions of residents, commuting workers, and tourists. It is like a human version of the New York Public Library. We can never know the story inside each person or book. Although the "covers" should not be judged, much can be imagined about what is inside. Candid photographs that freeze a person's demeanor, clothes, and expression provide clues. Similarly, the compositions, backgrounds, and details amplify these hints. As you look at the images in this chapter, what do you infer or feel? What meanings, symbols, and serendipities emerge?

To allow for interpretation, I typically only indicate the locations. Publishers require lengthier captions, but I did not want to skew your experience with literal descriptions. Instead, all captions in this book read as both a free-associative narrative inspired by the photographs and as individual standalone statements. Most of the images in this book were shot in or near Times Square, with two in Brooklyn (a New York City borough) and one in New Jersey. Photographs identified as "Times Square" are within a bowtie-shaped plaza where Broadway and 7th Avenue intersect, stretching between 42nd and 47th Streets. Otherwise, street names or addresses are provided.

These photographs were challenging to create—people rarely stayed still; there were distractions such as flashing billboard lights and a cacophony of noise; and I had to avoid getting hit by buses, falling victim to pickpockets, or crashing into tourists who came to a sudden stop. Another difficulty was the fear of pointing a camera at a stranger. My DSLR attracted attention. I might as well have been aiming a bazooka. My smartphone was inconspicuous. Some of those images appear in this book. Eventually, I settled on a professional point-and-shoot camera. Its small size made me as transparent as a ghost. The area between 51st Street and 34th Street became my haunting grounds with occasional excursions beyond.

As I photographed people with greater confidence, I kept thinking about how I was sticking a pin into their ambient bubbles of privacy. When artists surreptitiously create portraits, they risk being pilloried. Ironically, there are no widespread protests against the thousands of police cameras surveilling us in the city, the millions of smartphones enabling corporate tracking, and the hundreds of government imaging satellites orbiting the earth. These contradictions put me at ease about photographing people as a way of browsing the "library books." In America, entering a public space generally forfeits any reasonable expectation of privacy. The principle balances the right to privacy with the freedom of expression.

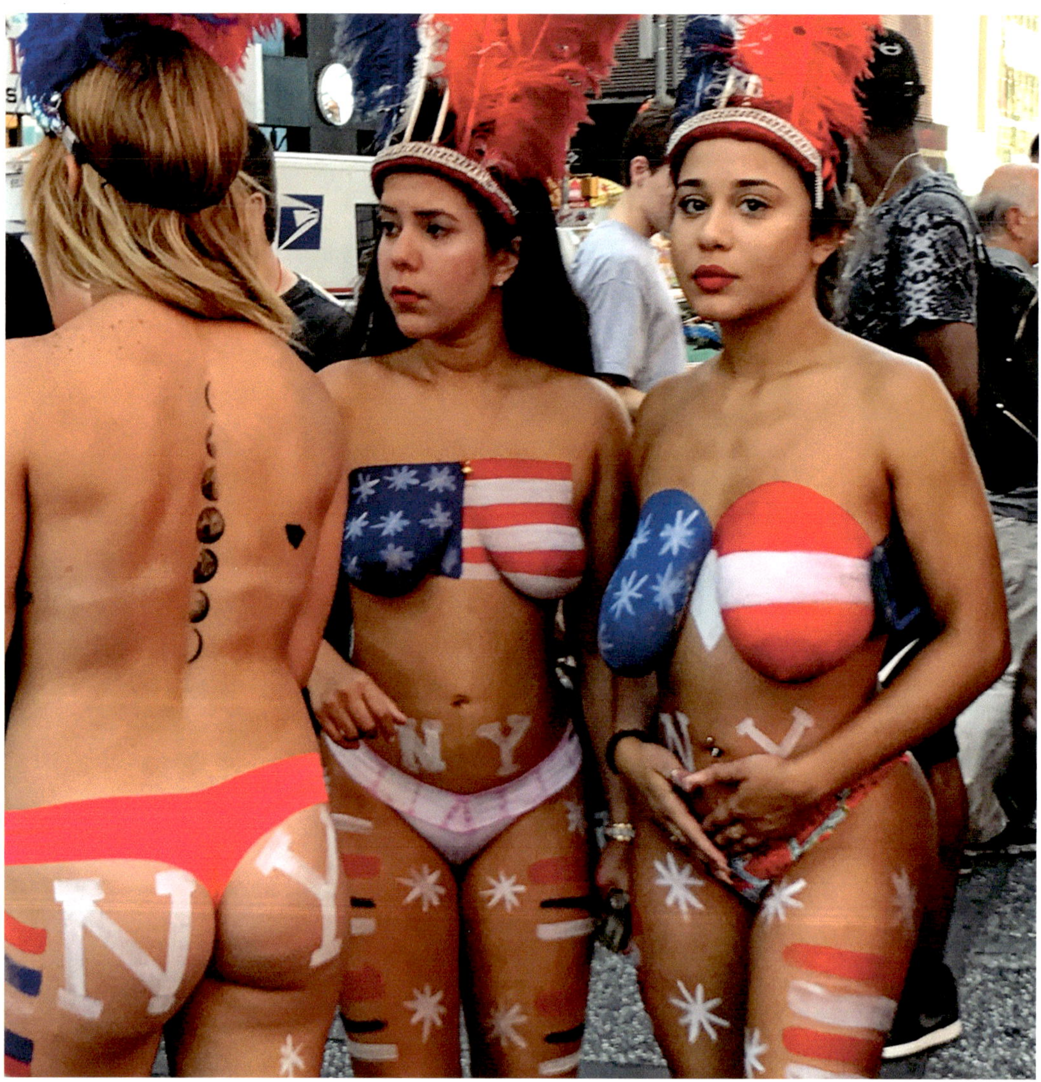

Manhattan, especially Times Square, can get crowded. The close proximity to strangers often causes anxiety and claustrophobia in some people. In this bustling environment, a photographer's accidental collision with the plumed tiara of a woman wearing patriotic body paint inspired a new artistic direction. (Times Square.)

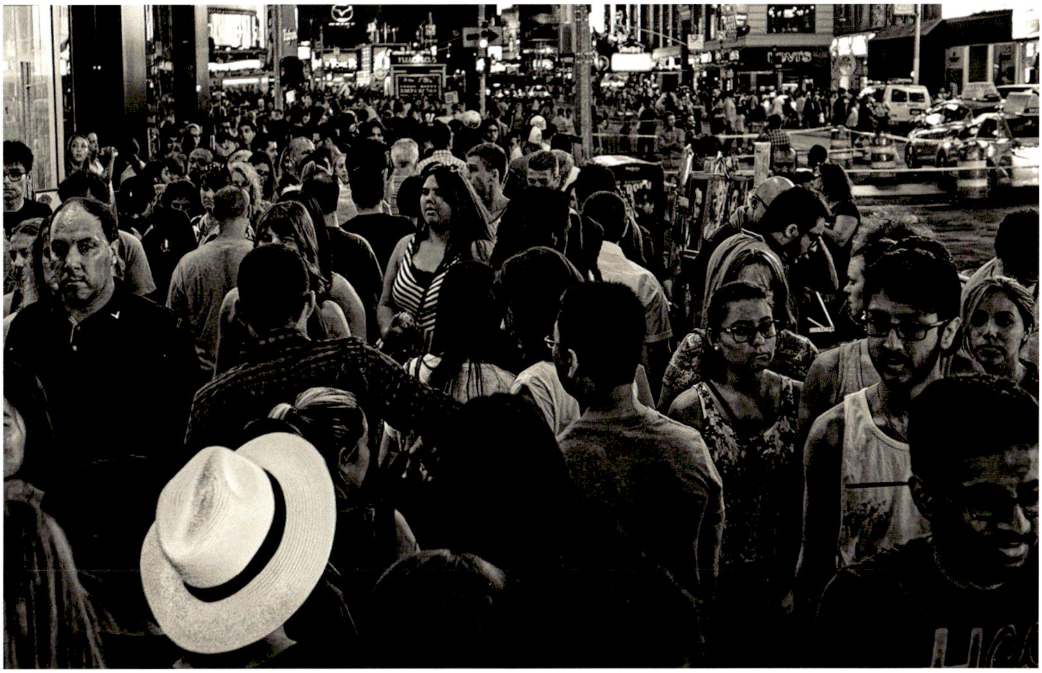

During a workday, the population can nearly double between the residents and the influx of nonresident workers and tourists. (Times Square.)

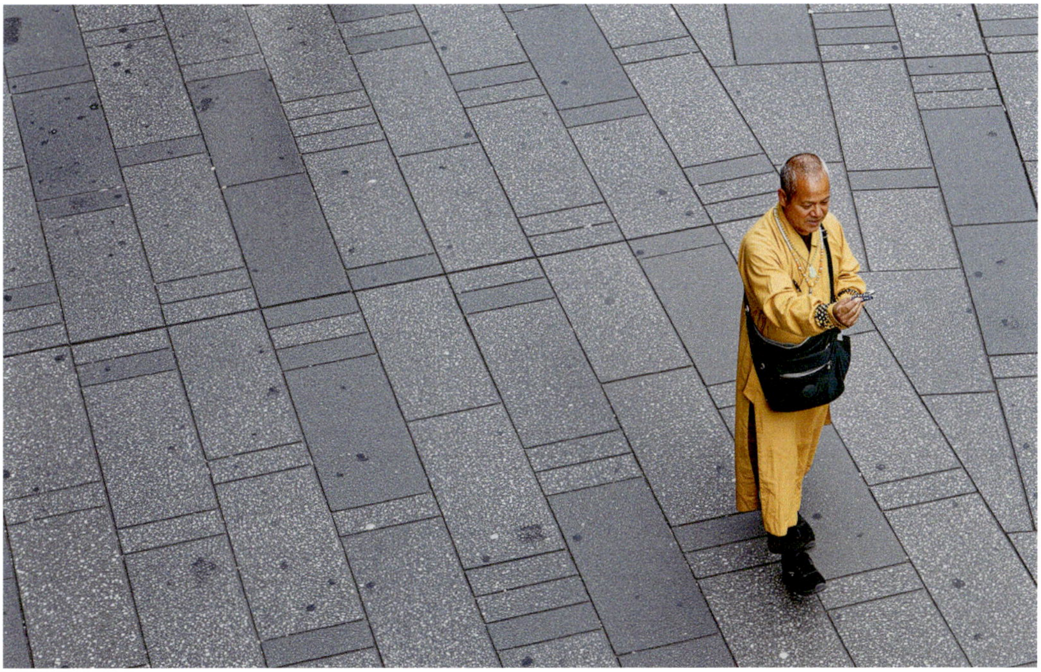

Although it is rare to be alone on the street, anonymity is common in urban life. Many people can still feel alone or isolated. (Times Square.)

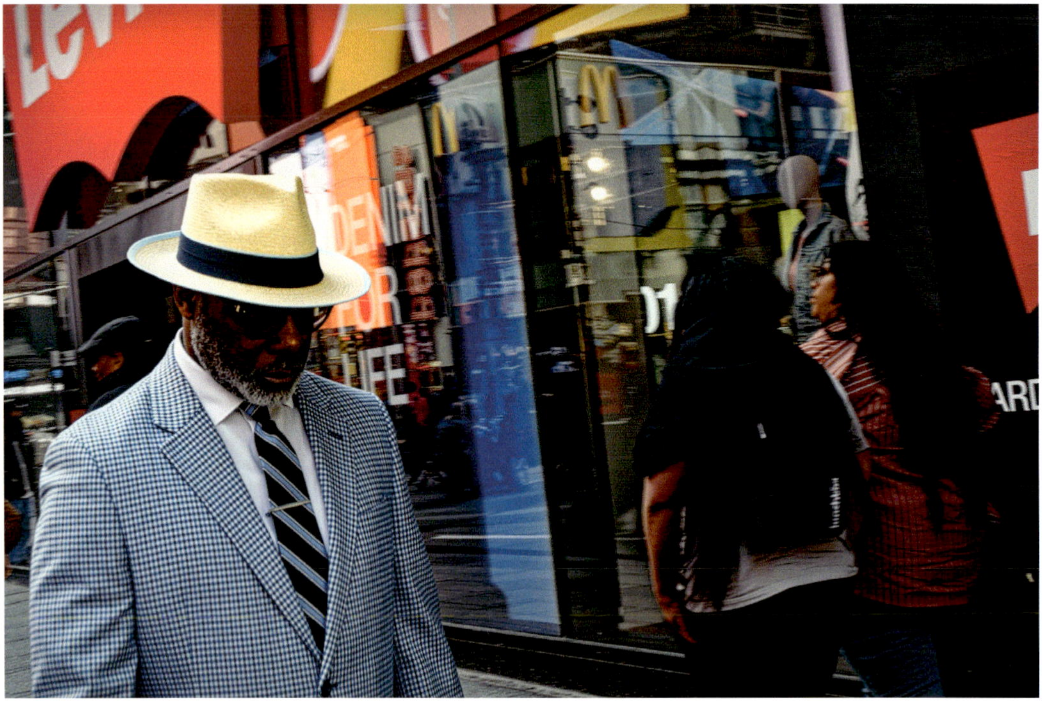

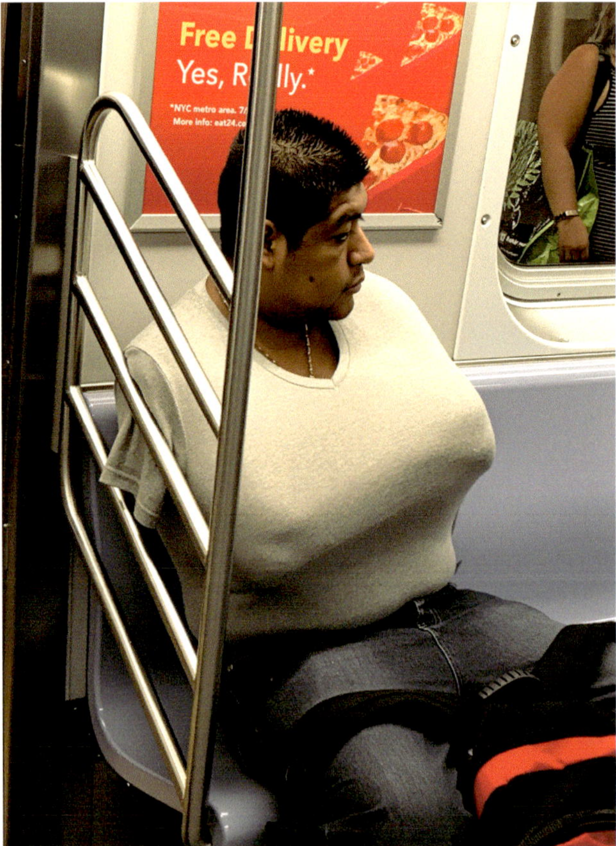

Above: After a while, the traffic, sirens, construction, music, and murmurs become a thrumming aural blanket, enveloping a pedestrian in deep thought. (Times Square.)

Left: Lost in reverie, it is easy to become unaware in an over-air-conditioned subway car. (F train at the "42nd Street-Bryant Park-Fifth Avenue" subway station.)

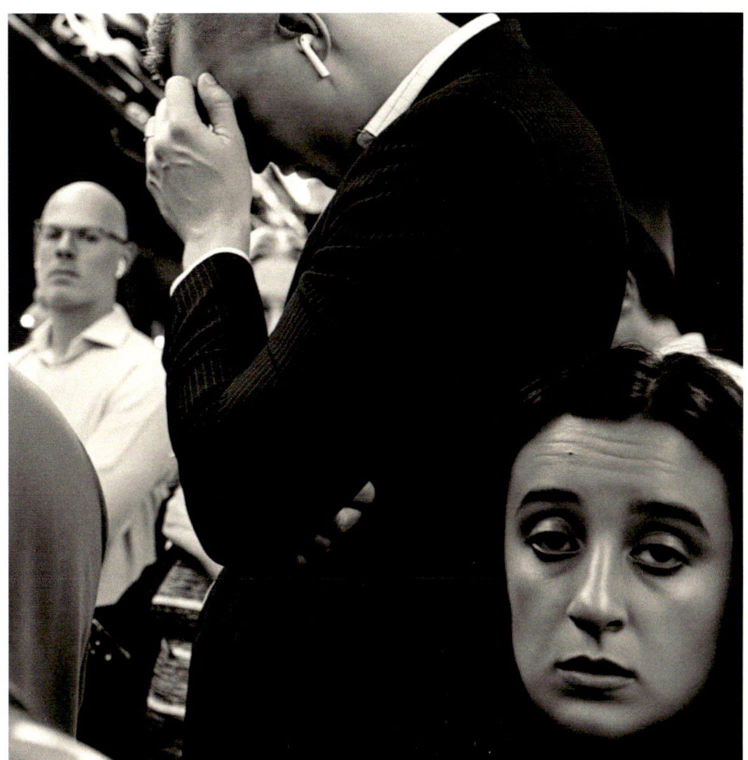

It is easy, as well, to lose patience waiting on a sweltering Long Island Railroad platform. Commuters get plunged into a private abyss of frustration and misery. (Track 18, Penn Station.)

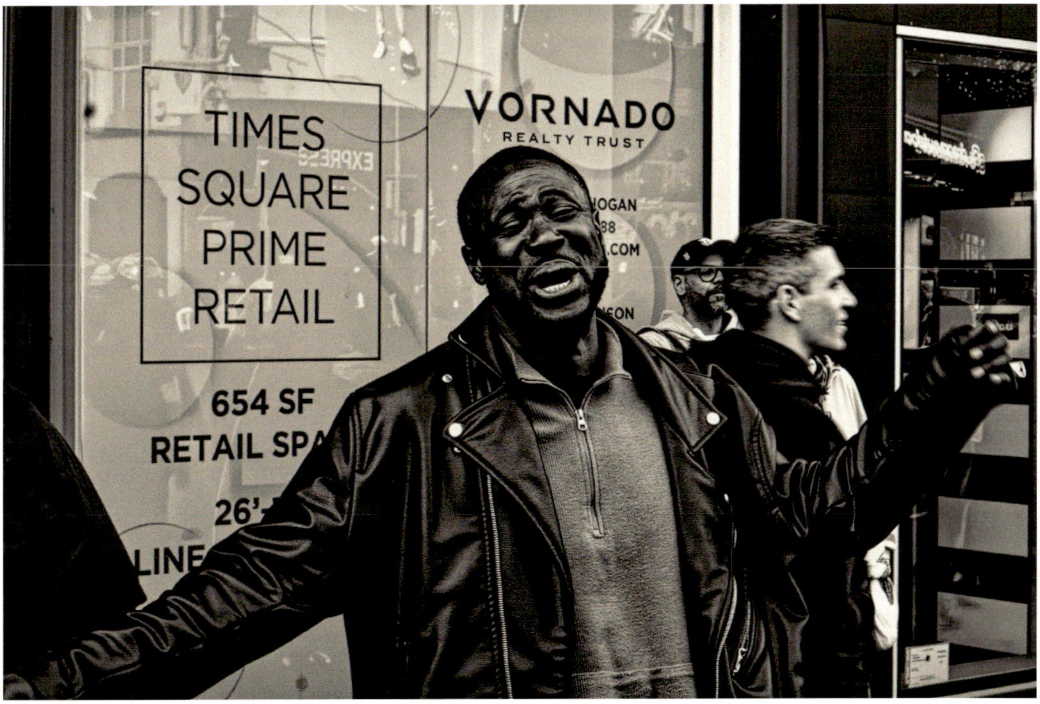

Others are engaged in a solitary struggle of the mind seeking attention or assistance from anyone who is willing to listen. (Times Square.)

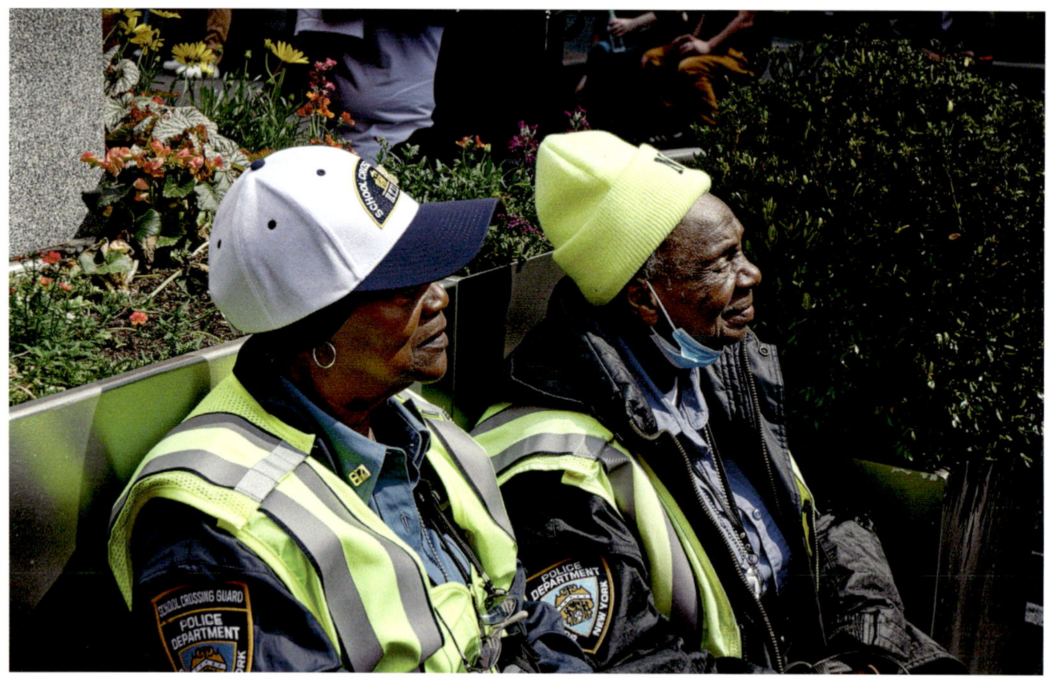

It is helpful to have a partner for camaraderie, sharing troubles and responsibilities, getting another point of view, and having back-up support. (Times Square.)

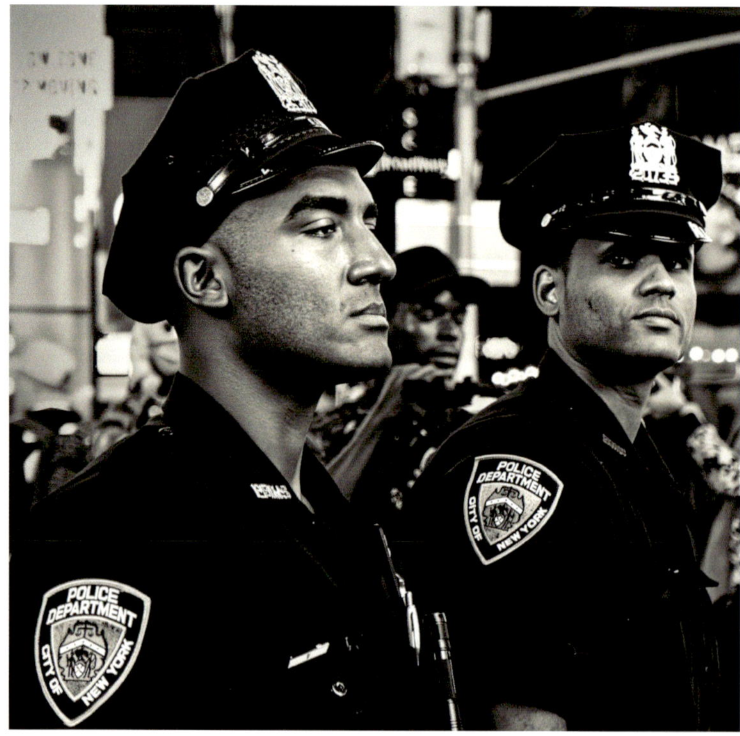

New York's finest often pair up in areas like Times Square, which attracts political protests and has occasionally been the site of violent incidents, including shootings, stabbings, a machete assault, and thwarted terrorist plots. (Times Square.)

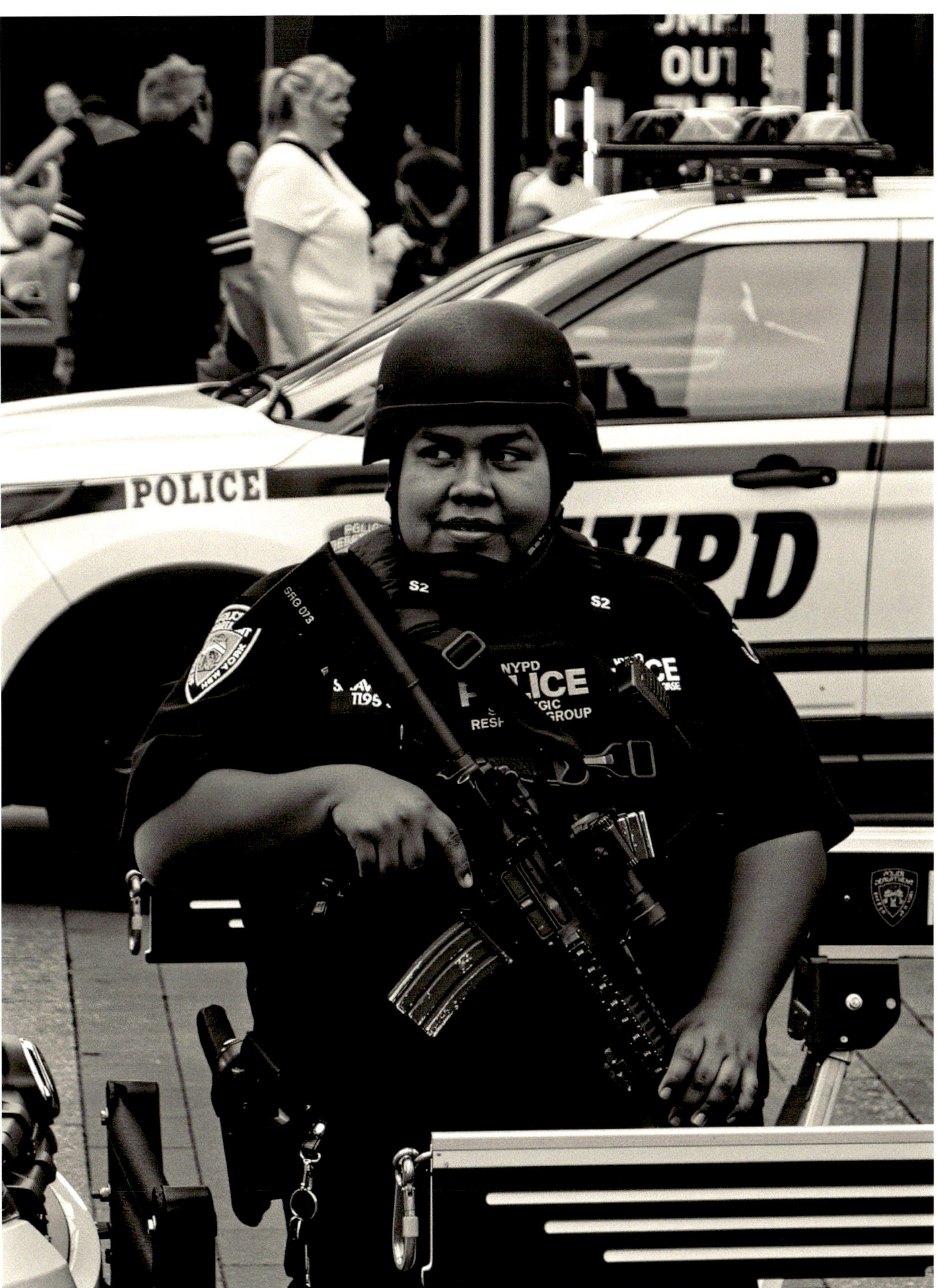

Sometimes such a high-profile location needs an equally high-profile companion: a powerful state-of-the-art rifle. The New York City Police Department's Strategic Response Group was formed in 2015 to combat terrorism, control crowds during protests, and respond to emergencies. (Times Square.)

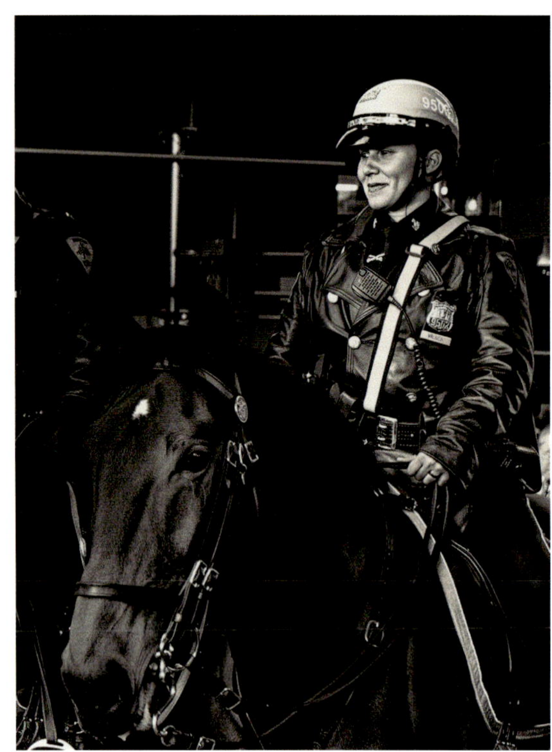

The horse may be a low-tech teammate, but it offers an ideal advantage for the Mounted Unit, which was established in 1858. The elevated position enables officers to see over crowds and deters potential wrongdoers when they see the mounted cop. It can also be easier and quicker to navigate through dense crowds than on foot or in vehicles. (Times Square.)

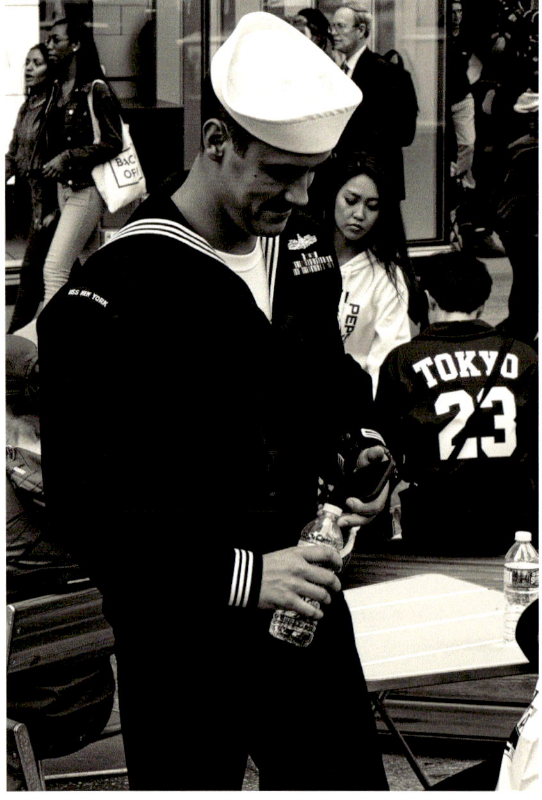

The police do not work alone. While sailors, soldiers, and airmen defend the nation, the NYPD and the FBI work closely with the New York National Guard's Joint Task Force Empire Shield. The JTF-ES is the state's standing military organization to defend against terrorism. (Times Square.)

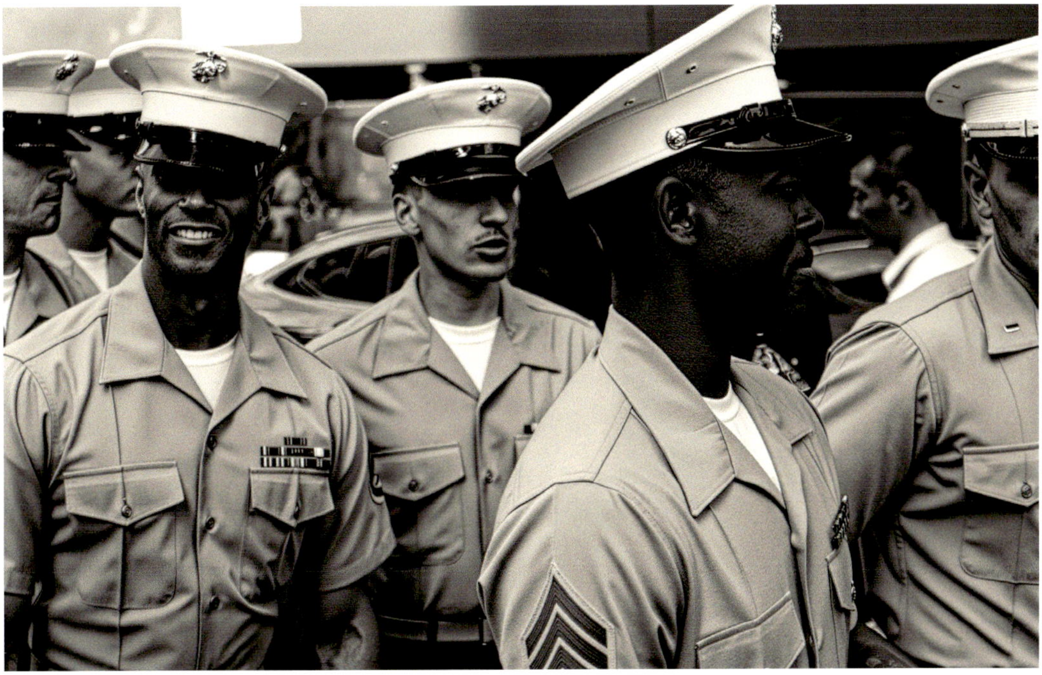

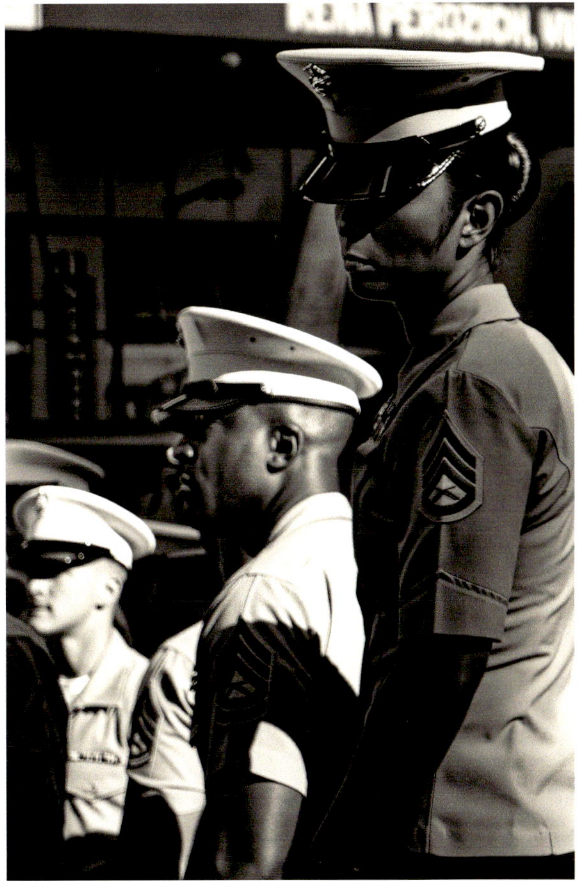

Above: To honor those who serve the country, the city hosts its annual Fleet Week, a Memorial Day celebration that welcomes over 2,000 members of the U.S. Marine Corps, Navy, and Coast Guard. (Times Square.)

Right: The sight of these military uniforms, as well as those of the police, presents an interesting contrast with the fashion sensibility of the civilians they protect. (Times Square.)

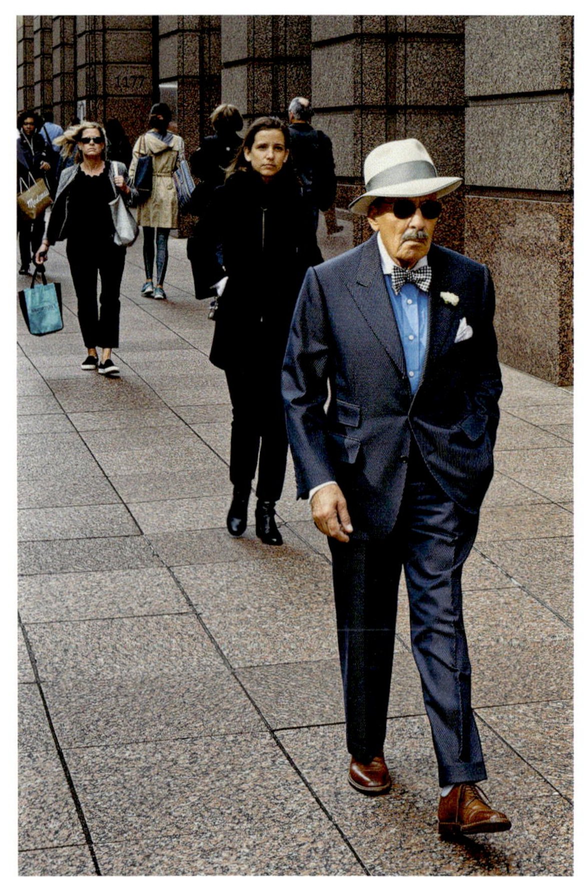

Left: Originally an Italian military police officer, Domenico Spano, seen here in a dapper suit, hat, and sunglasses, would later be hailed by *The New York Times* as a "clothier of the stars." The price of Spano's suits started at around $6,000. He loved the classic American look of Fred Astaire, Cary Grant, and Gary Cooper. (1177 6th Avenue.)

Below: Hats and sunglasses are a popular way of completing an outfit. The fedora is not only an elegant accessory for men, but for smartly dressed women as well. (7th Avenue at West 40th Street.)

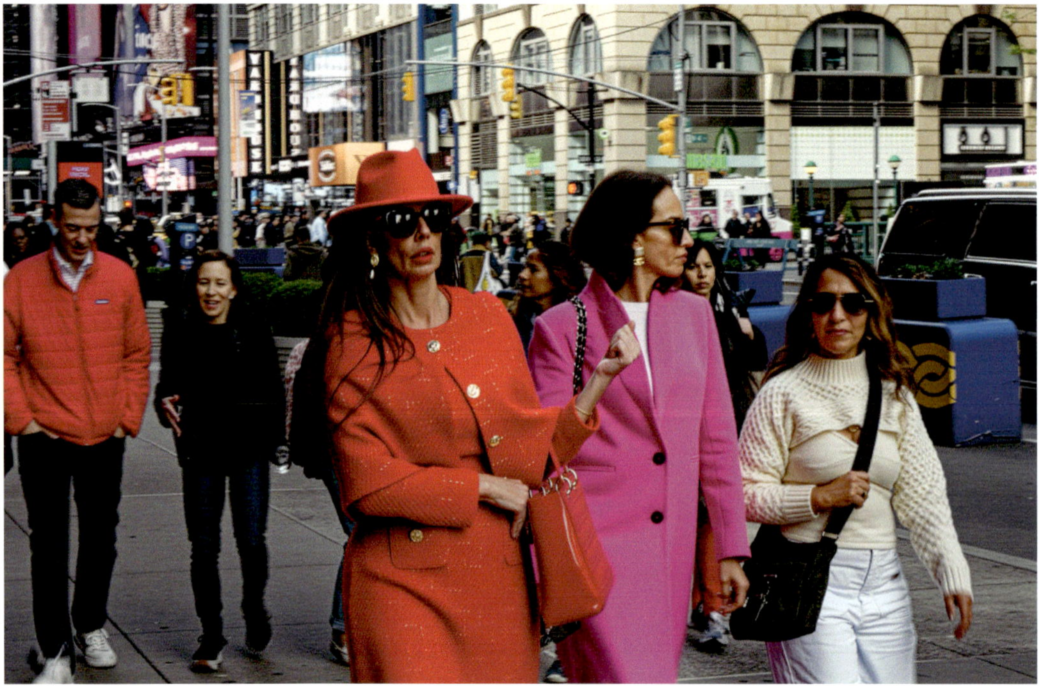

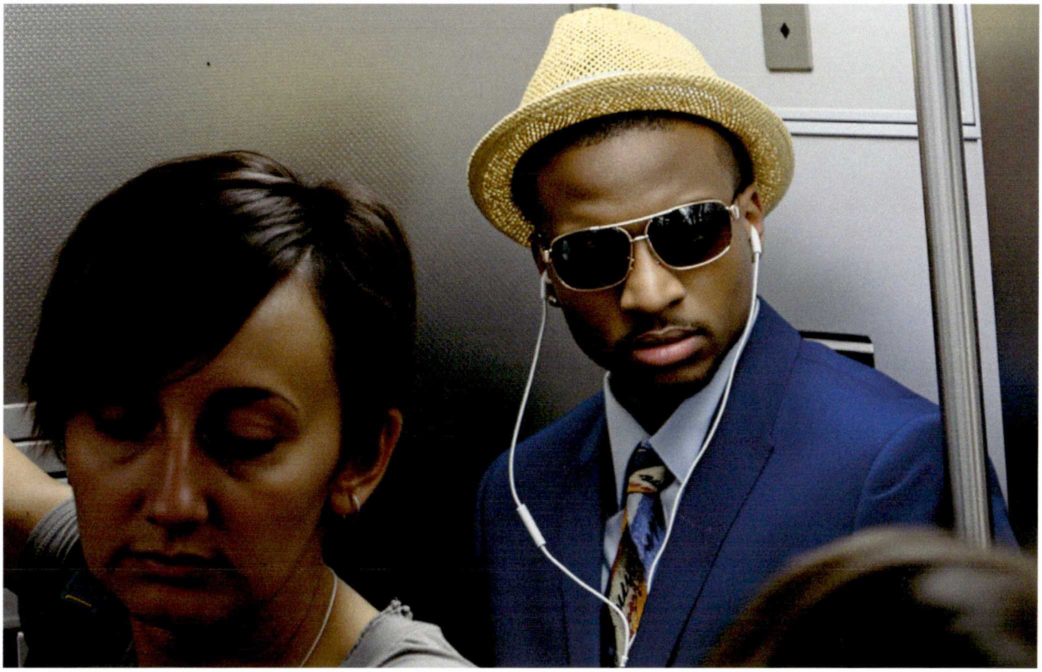

This well-appointed young man sports a sophisticated vintage vibe that would not be out of place in a cool jazz or ska setting. (E train, subway.)

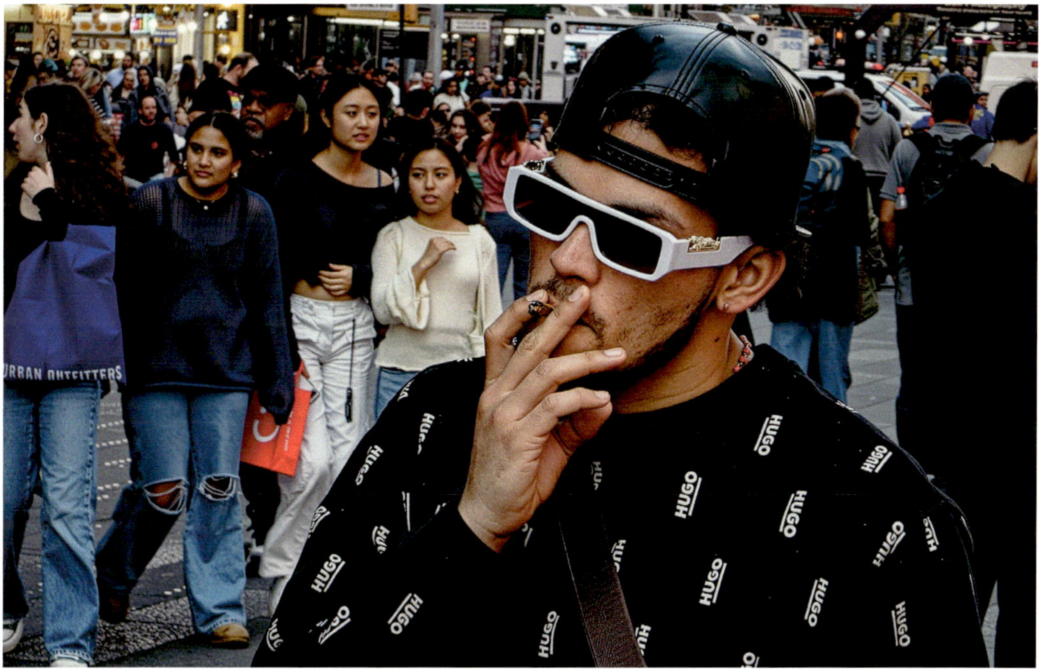

For a contemporary "New York tough" sensibility, the hip hop street fashion of a backwards cap with designer clothes is *de rigueur*. (Times Square.)

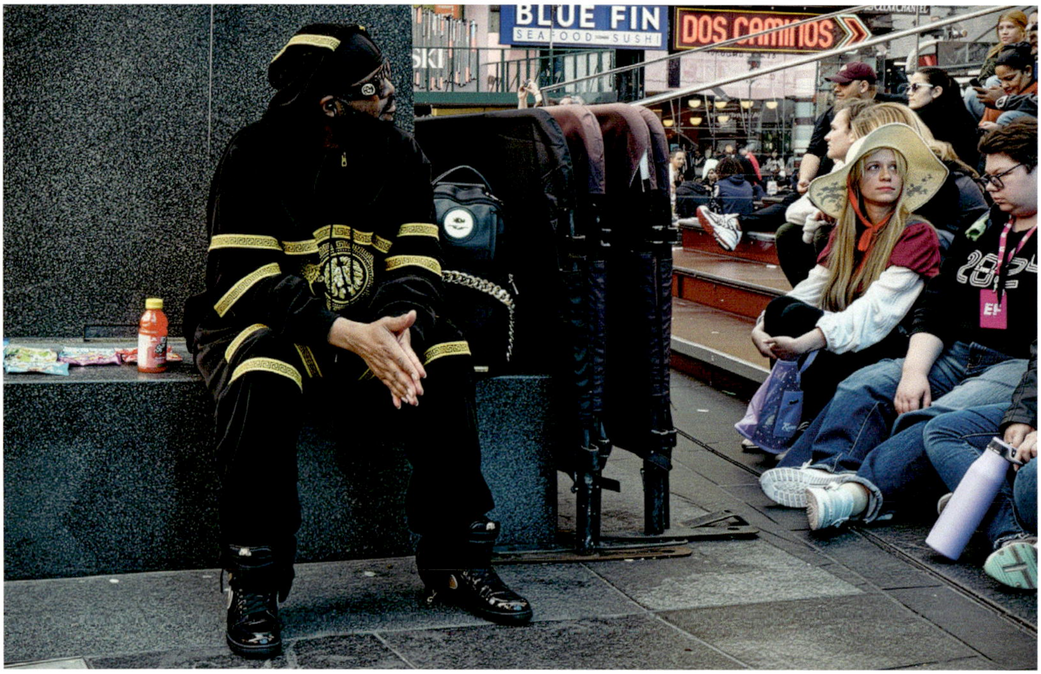

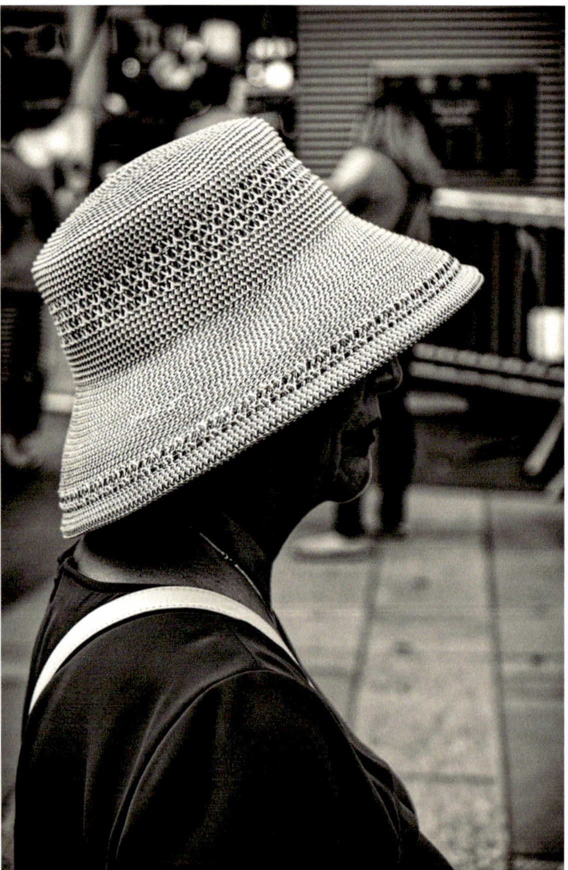

Above: Some prefer to dispense with a hat in favor of a hoodie and durag. When coupled with a black shirt, black pants, gold trim, and a lion emblem, the result is quite unique and regal. (TKTS Red Steps, Times Square.)

Left: The flipside is to skip the sunglasses and opt for a sun hat to create a relaxed and comfortable ensemble. It is ideal for places like Times Square where visitors will be hard-pressed to find any tree shade. (Times Square.)

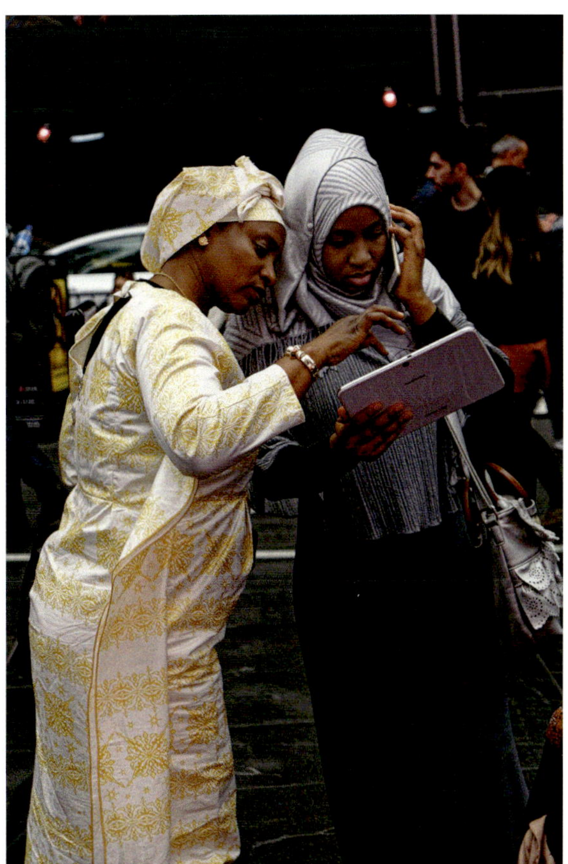

Right: The variety of clothing from different cultures contributes to the vibrant tapestry of New York City's street life. (Times Square.)

Below: It does not always have to be a conventional western hat. An African headwrap is a powerful symbol of heritage, identity, and pride. (Times Square.)

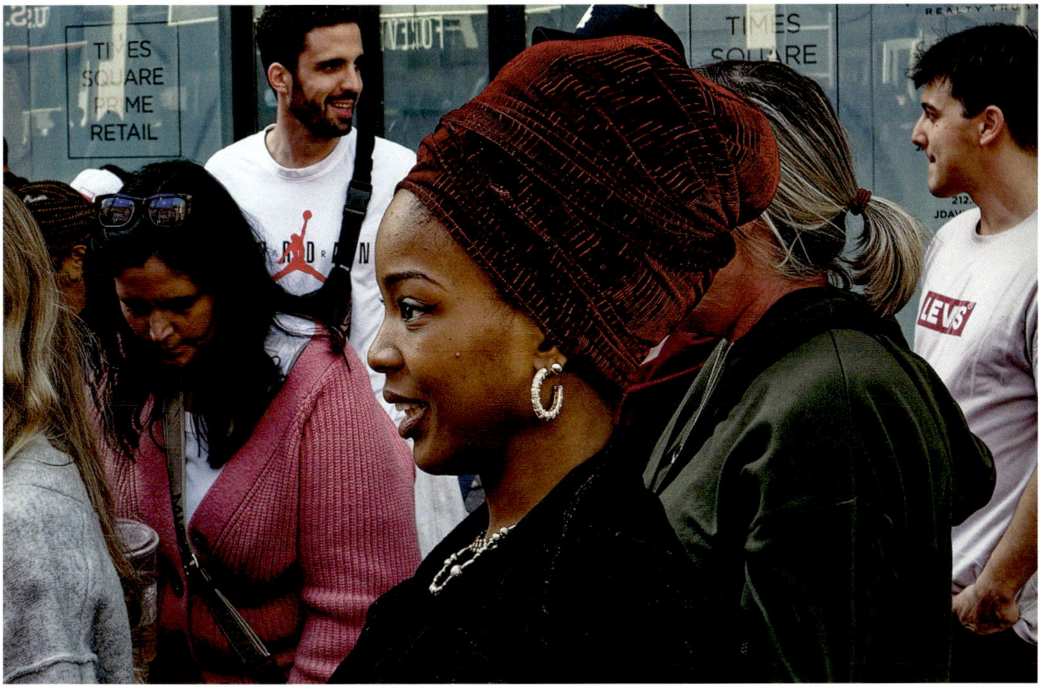

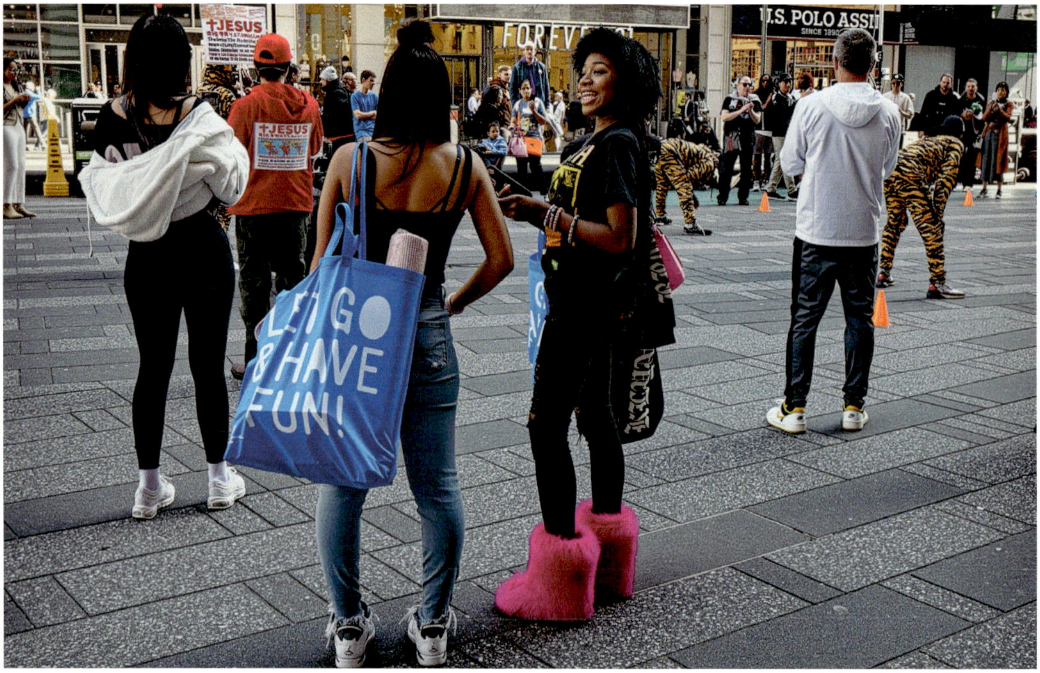

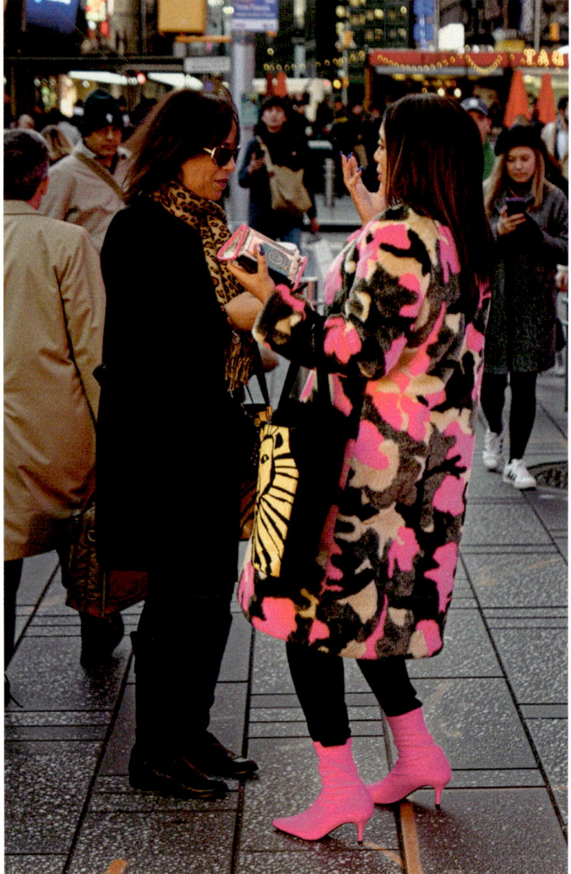

Above: Going down the opposite direction is another important element: footwear. Faux fur boots are a soft, comfortable, and trendy attention-getter. (Times Square.)

Left: For a bolder statement, color-coordinating a flamboyant jacket with boots is another way to stand out in a crowd. (Times Square.)

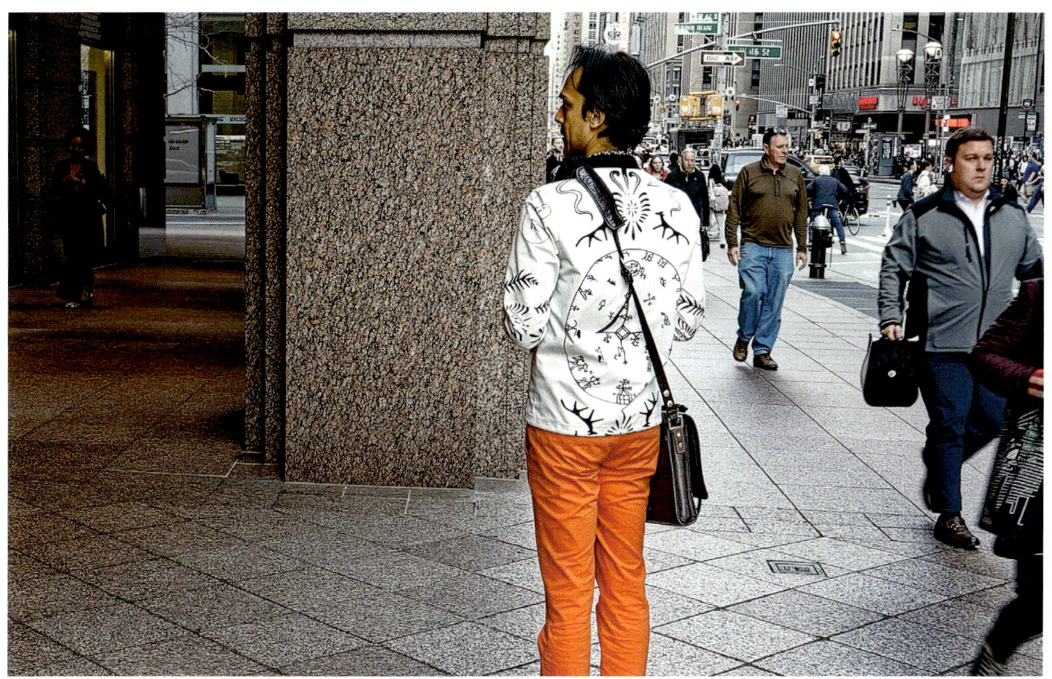

Men can also playfully assert their individuality. Many have moved away from the corporate conformity and conventionality of gray flannel or blue pin-stripe suits. (1177 6th Avenue.)

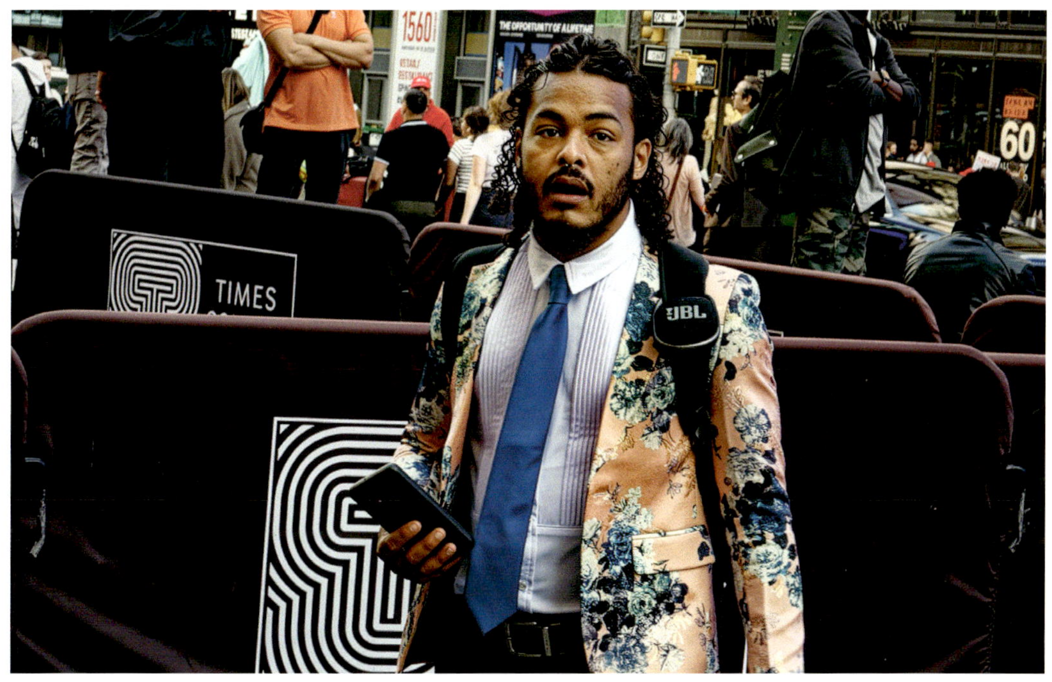

New York is an artful stage, showcasing a relaxed confidence. A distinctive pattern of blue flowers makes a pink jacket pop. (7th Avenue at West 46th Street.)

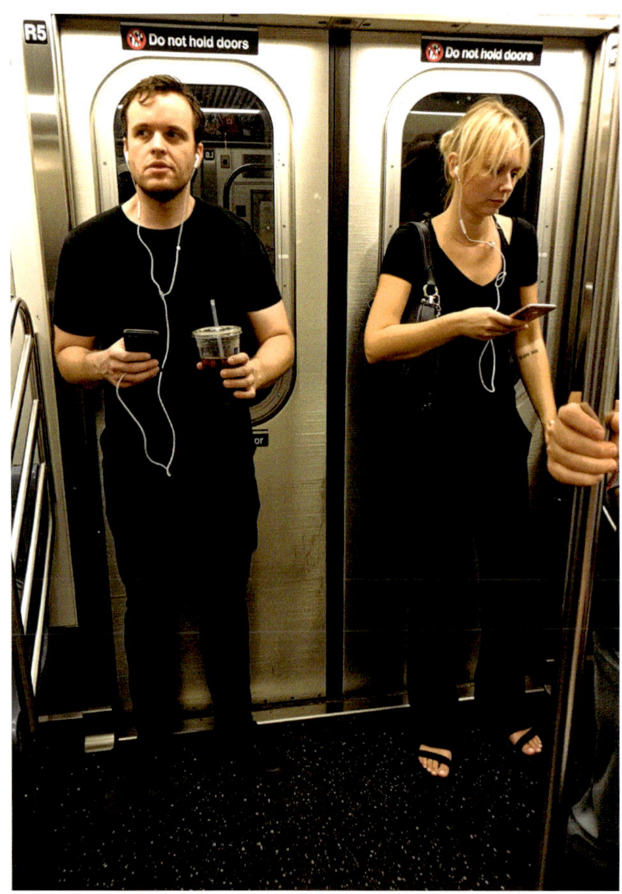

Left: These two, who were apparently strangers to each other, happened to be dressed in all-black, which was popular when the city was home to large nightclubs like Sound Factory, the Limelight, and the Tunnel. (7 train, subway.)

Below: New Yorkers possess a distinct quality arising in part from the mix of native residents and multicultural newcomers from across the nation and around the world. ("Lexington Avenue/51 Street" subway station.)

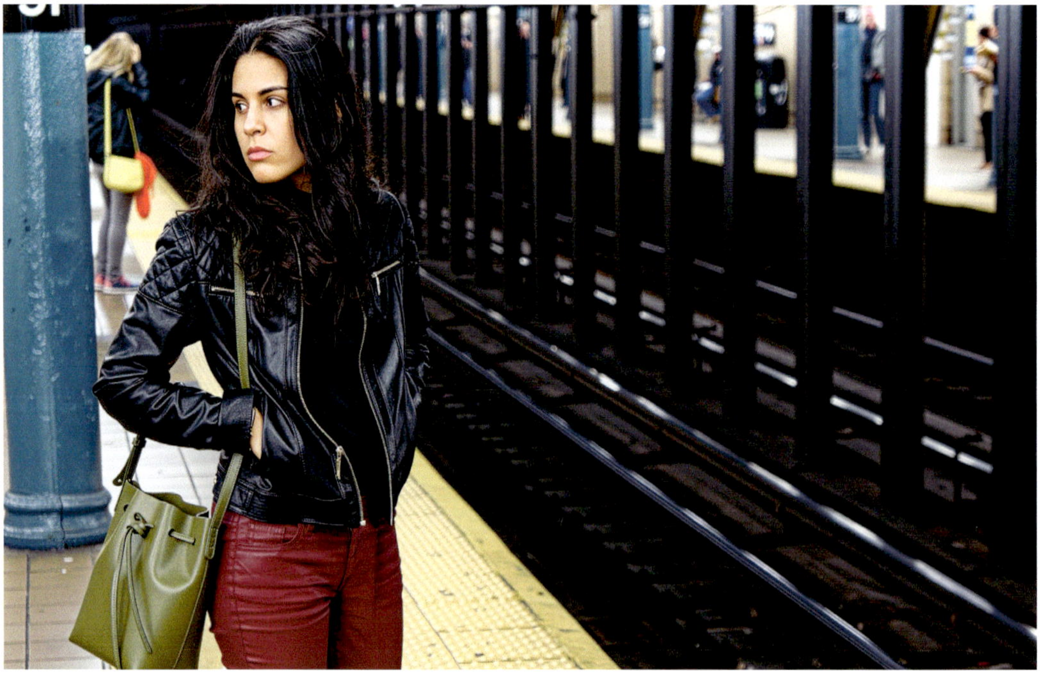

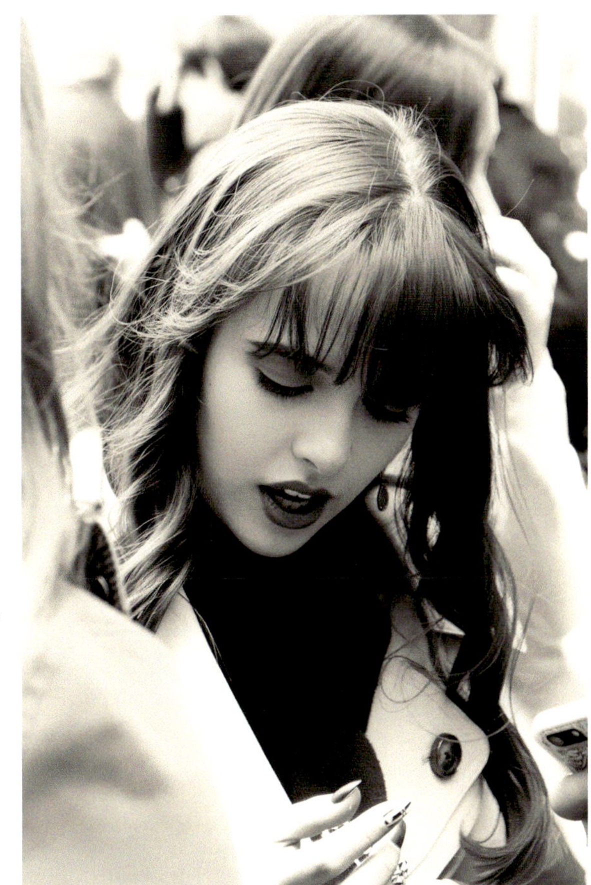

Right: The diversity ensures a constantly evolving mix of high-end designer clothes, uniforms, business attire, streetwear, and many combinations that defy description. (Broadway Theater District.)

Below: As New York City is a style capital, perhaps it was no coincidence that the musical *Hair* debuted here in 1967 and won the Tony Award in 2009 when it returned to Broadway. (Times Square.)

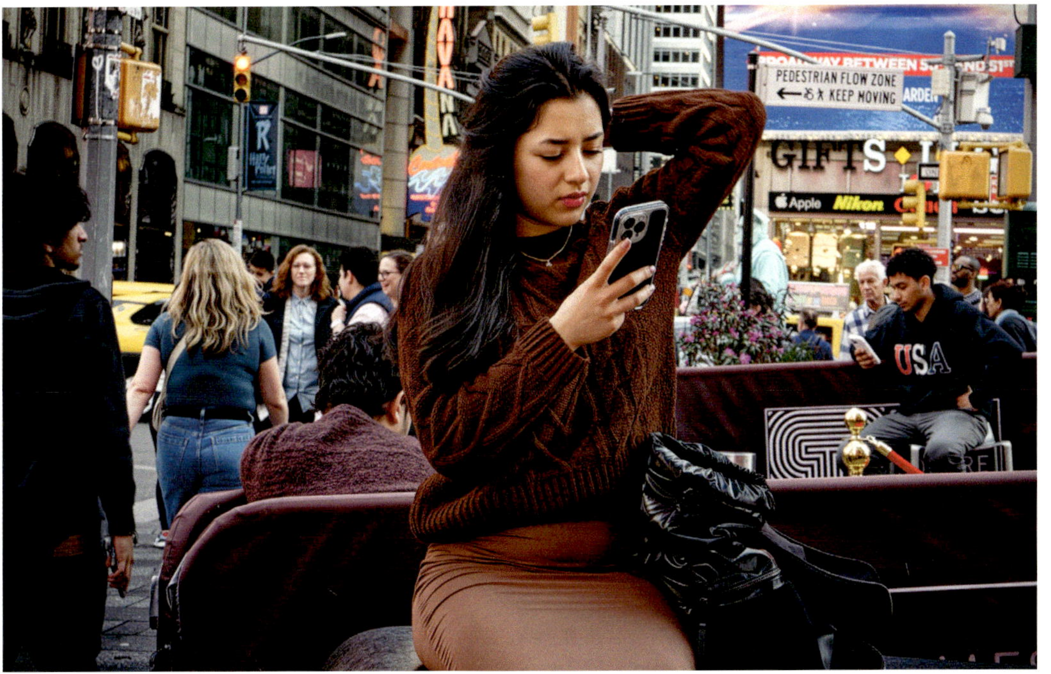

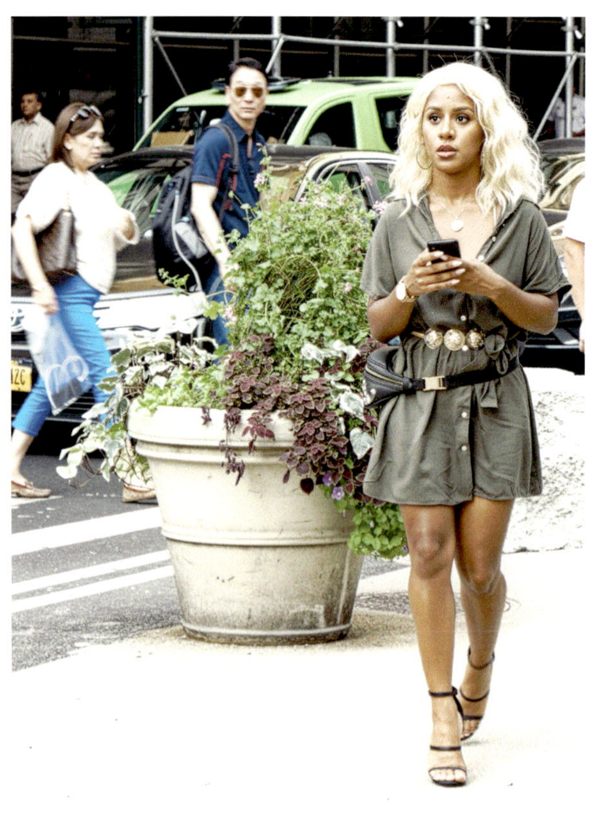

As heard in the titular song from *Hair*, there are "no words for the beauty and the splendor." (Greeley Square Park, 6th Avenue at West 33rd Street.)

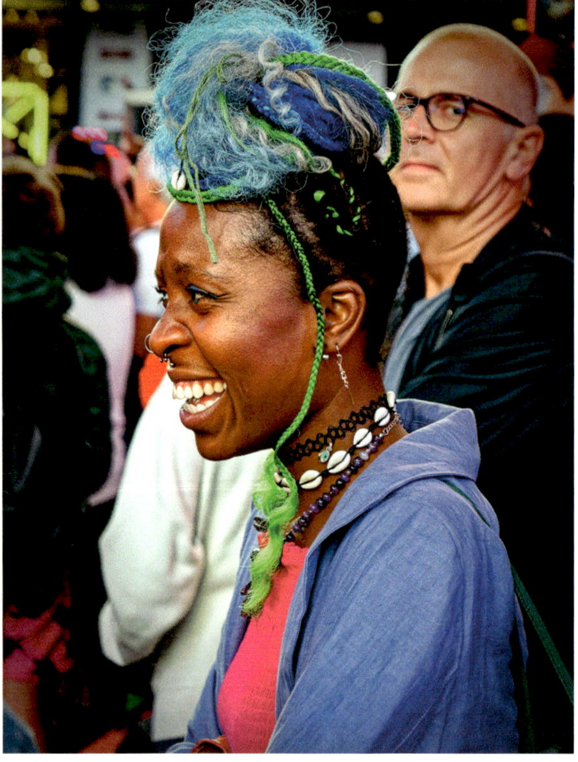

The wide range of how hair is worn, especially for women, is as extensive as that of clothing and accessories. (Times Square.)

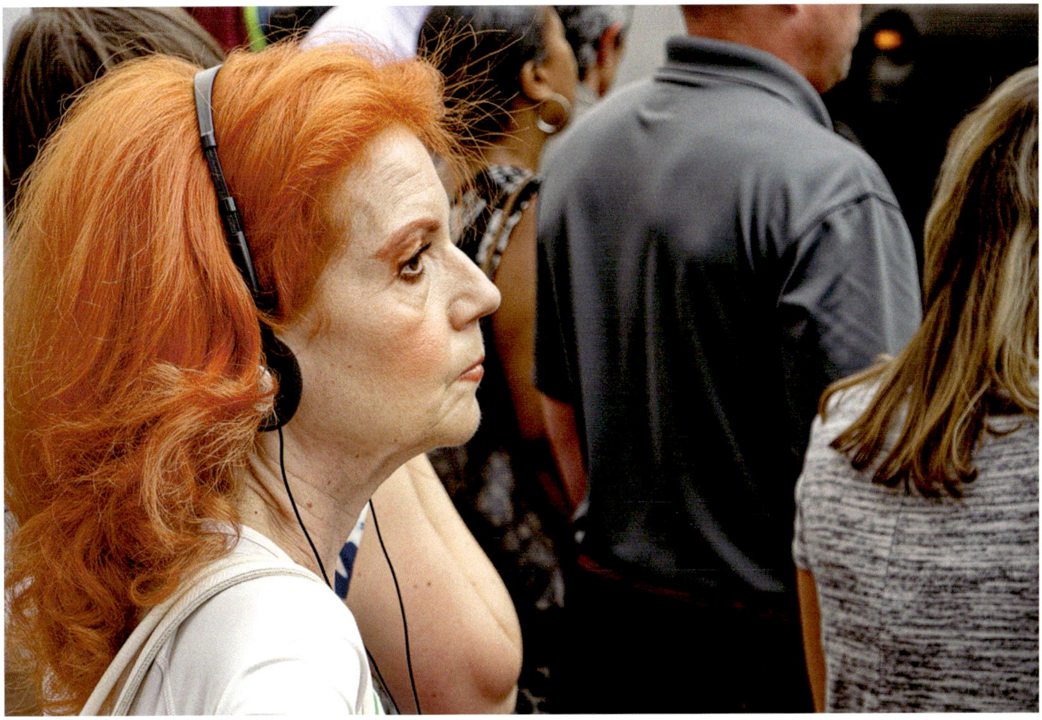

Above: Hairstyles, particularly in major cities like New York, have undergone significant transformations throughout the twentieth and twenty-first centuries. (West 34th Street at 7th Avenue.)

Right: Nowadays, many women wear their hair long. In the early 1900s, the Gibson Girl bouffant, with the locks piled high on top of the head, was all the rage and embodied a new spirit of independence. (Broadway at 36th Street.)

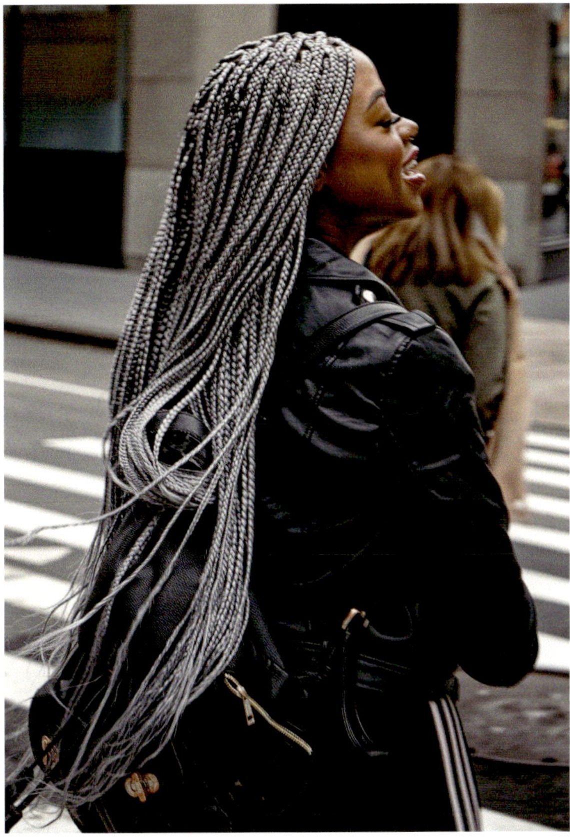

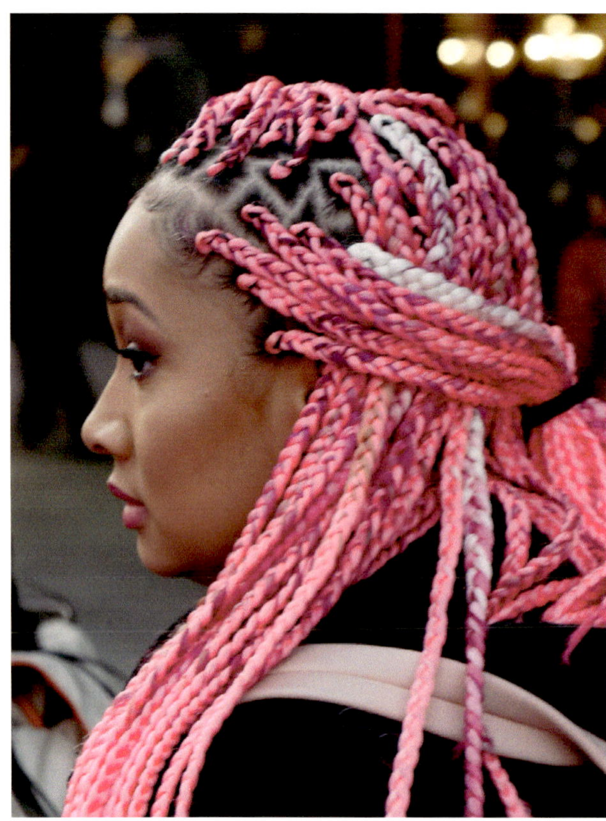

By the 1920s, the freedom and rebellion of the Jazz Age gave rise to the short bob. Over the decades, both short and long hair have come in and out of fashion, with varying styles based on straight, wavy, curled, and, as pictured here, braided hair. (Times Square.)

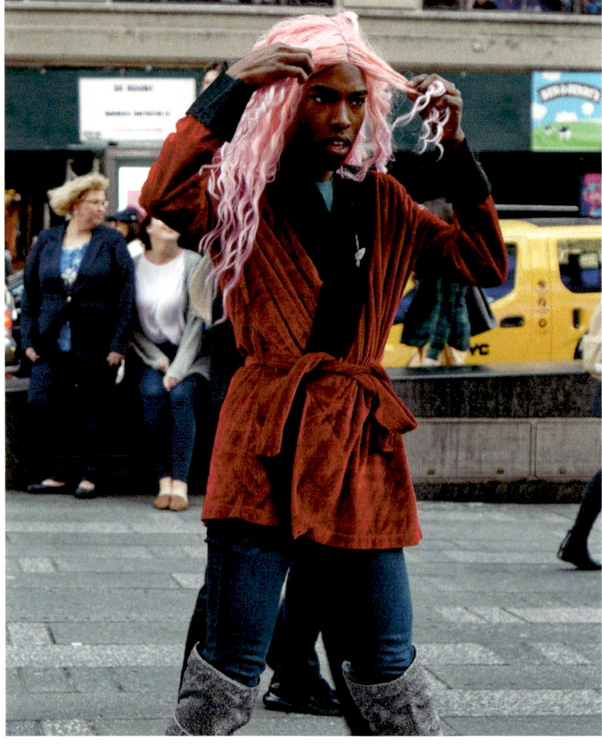

Starting in the 1950s, wigs and extensions steadily gained popularity as new washable synthetic materials were developed. (Times Square.)

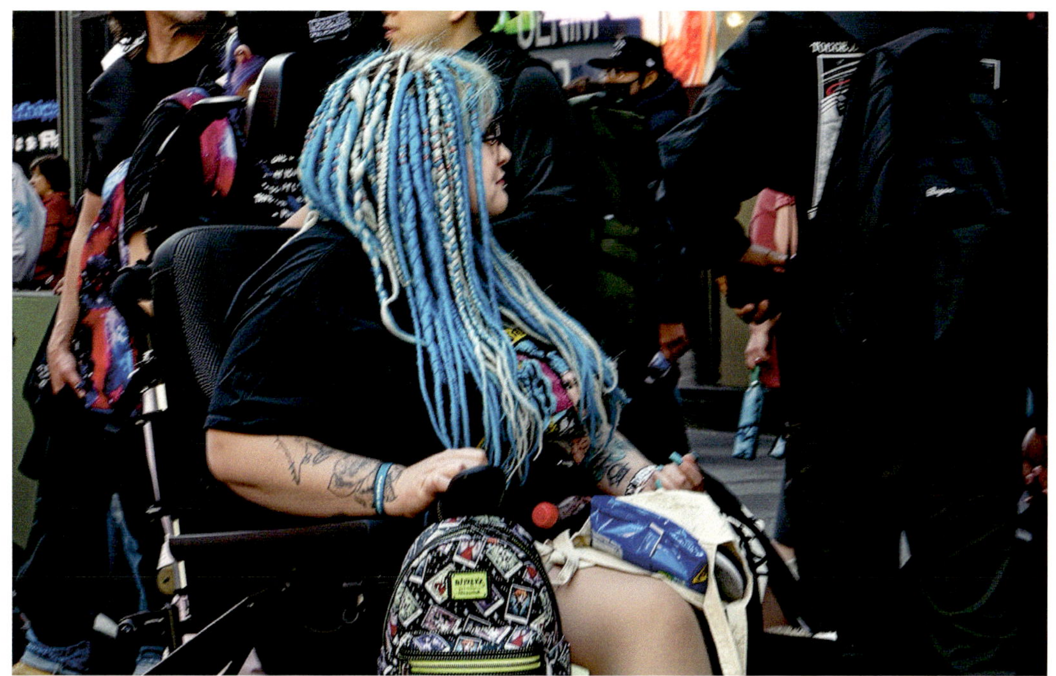

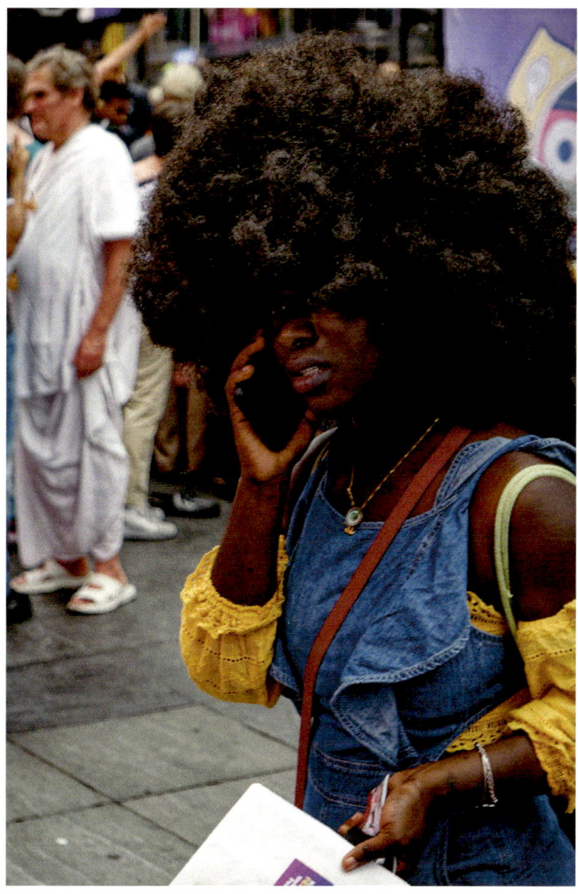

Above: Other postwar improvements were made in dyes and formulations, which introduced bright alternative colors that gained greater acceptance during the rise of punk rock in mid-1970s Manhattan. (Times Square.)

Right: Although by the 1980s the afro was starting to decline in popularity, it continues to resonate today as a cultural shift away from trying to conform to white beauty standards. (Times Square.)

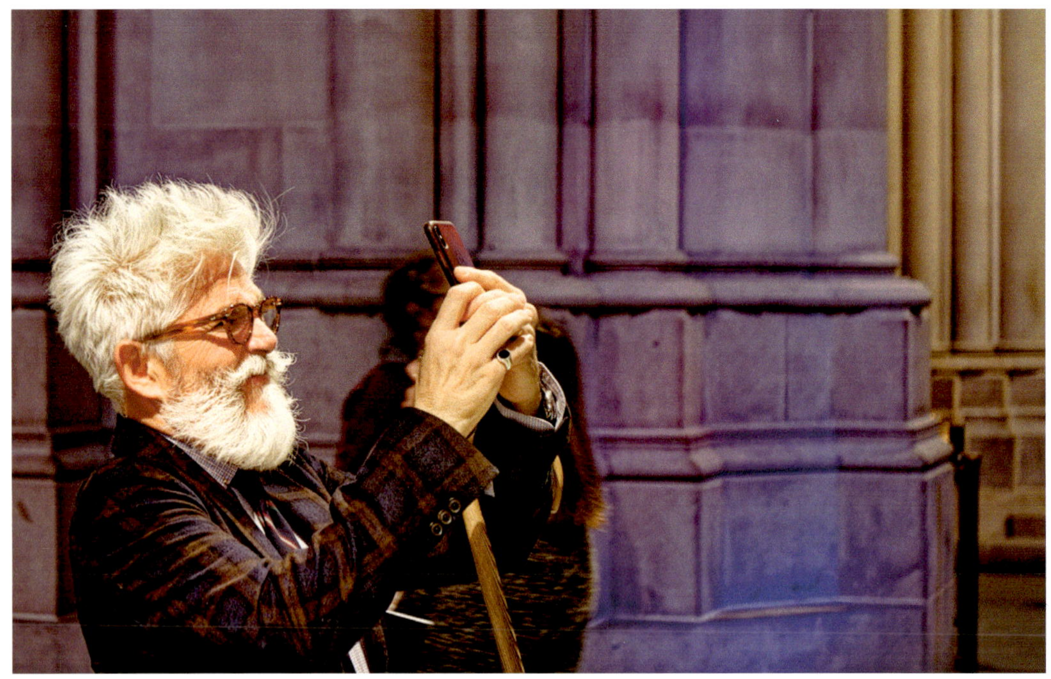

Above: For men, short hair and a clean-shaven face predominated for much of the last century. The contemporary panoply of longer, wilder hair, mustaches, beards, and sideburns can be traced back to the 1960s counterculture. (The Cathedral Church of Saint John the Divine.)

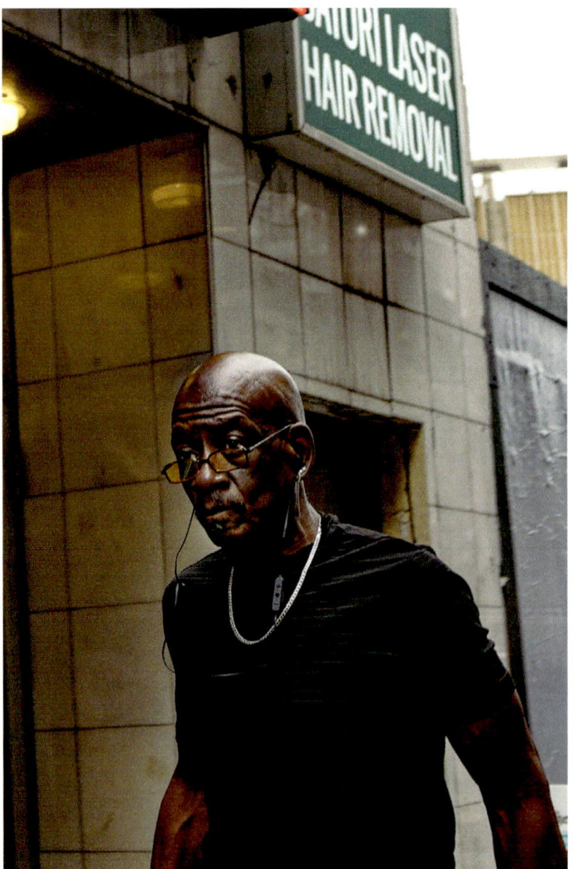

Left: The most dramatic change was the mainstream acceptance of baldness. Early adopters like Yul Brynner in the 1950s, and Isaac Hayes and Telly Savalas in the 1970s, brought attention to the look. By the 1990s, more men followed the trend as a new generation of celebrities shaved their heads. The appearance of the "Hair Removal" sign in the photograph is completely serendipitous. (8th Avenue at 34th Street.)

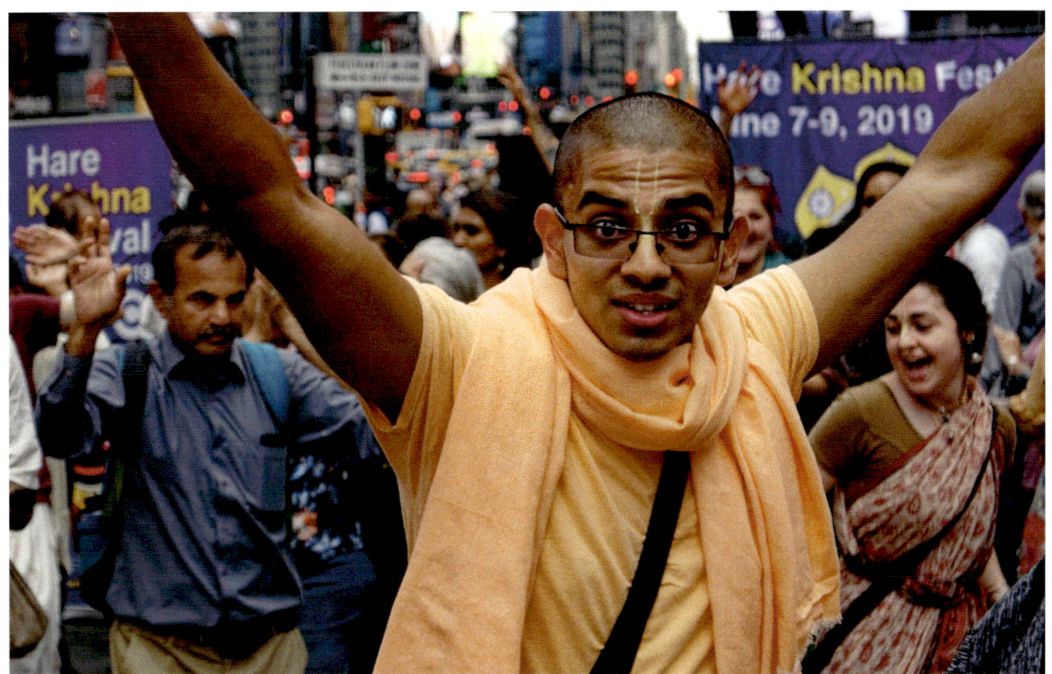

Shaved heads are commonly observed among men who are devotees of the Hare Krishna movement. Rather than a fashion statement, this practice symbolizes detachment from outward appearance and material vanity. (Ratha Yatra Festival, Times Square.)

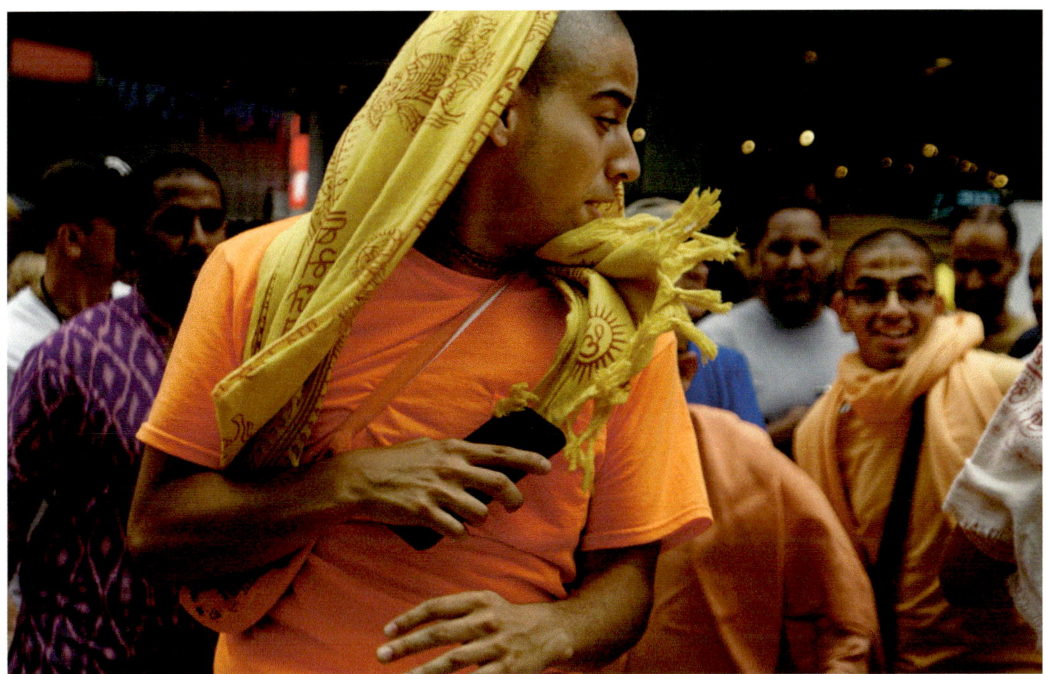

The first Hare Krishna temple outside of India was established in 1966 in Manhattan's East Village and initially attracted many white hippies. Since then, it has gained followers among the growing Hindu diaspora in New York City. (Ratha Yatra Festival, Times Square.)

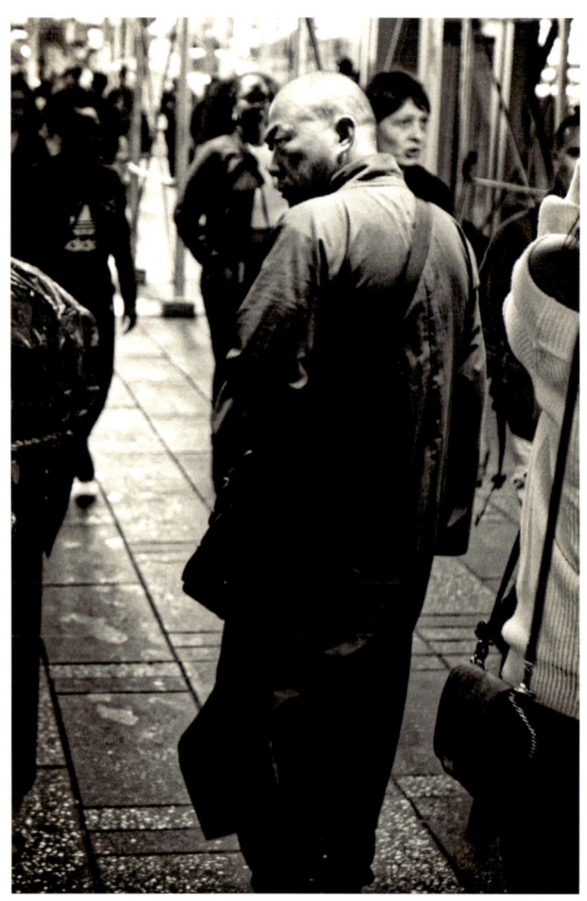

Left: Not all hairless men in orange robes are legitimate. The Parks Department and Buddhist leaders have warned of fake monks bearing gifts. These impostors often push a paper tchotchke into people's hands or place beads on women's wrists, then aggressively demand cash. (Times Square.)

Below: Sometimes, it can be hard to distinguish whether an outfit is a costume or a daring fashion experiment. (Times Square.)

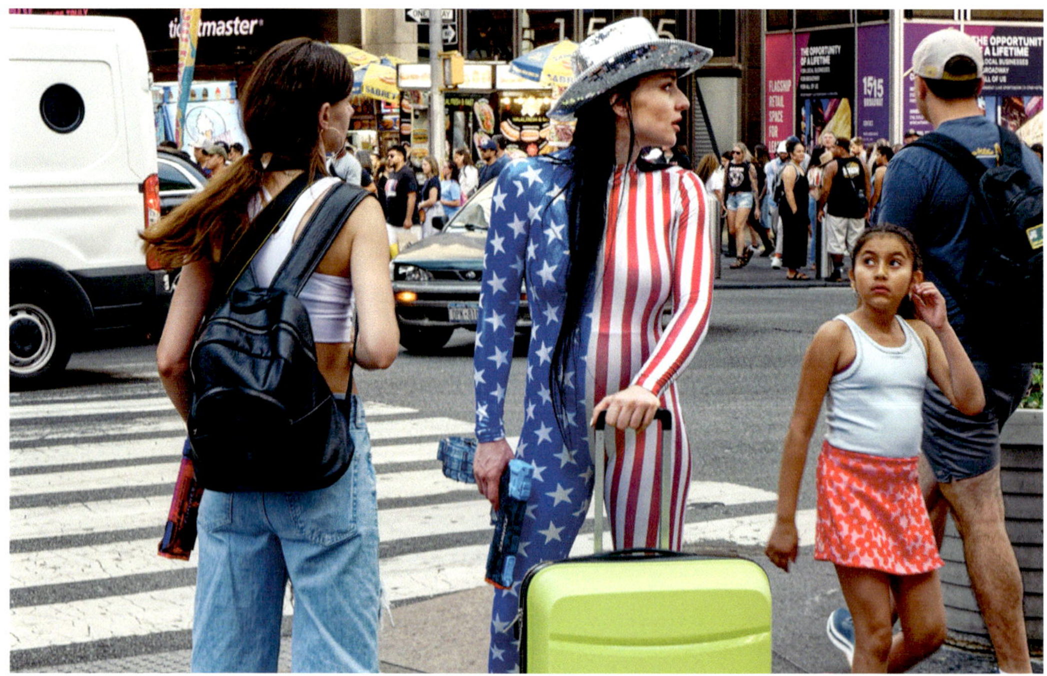

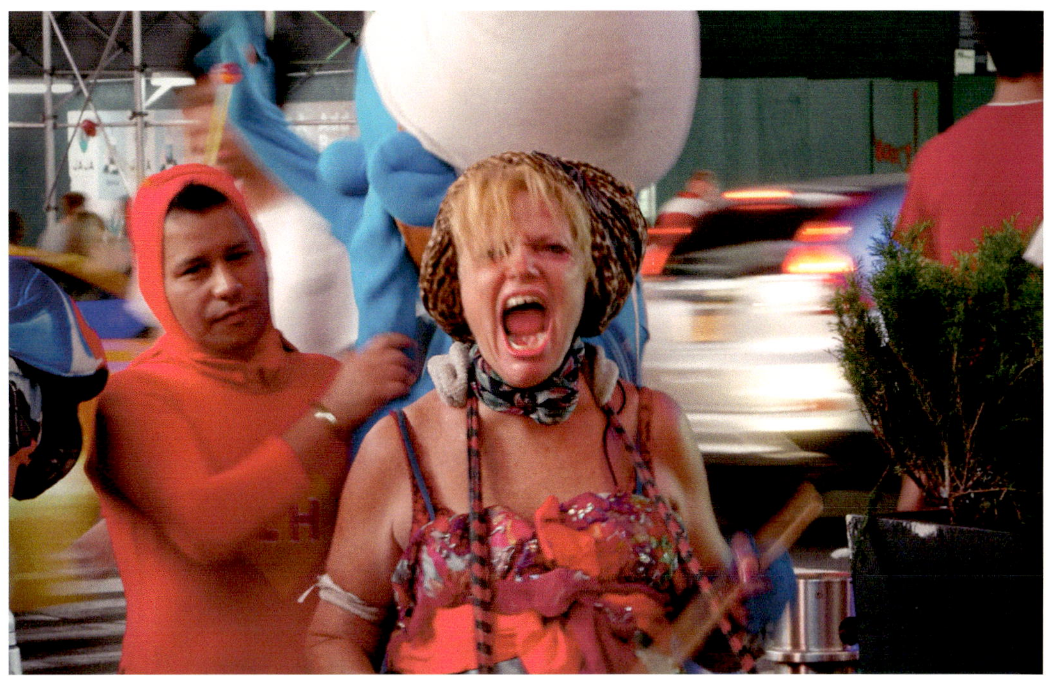

Other times, it is easy to recognize a getup, even when identifying the character proves challenging. The man in red is dressed as "El Chapulín Colorado," a comedic Mexican superhero. While *chapulines* (toasted grasshoppers) have yet to gain popularity with Yankees or Mets fans, they are a favored concession snack at the Seattle Mariners' baseball stadium. (Times Square.)

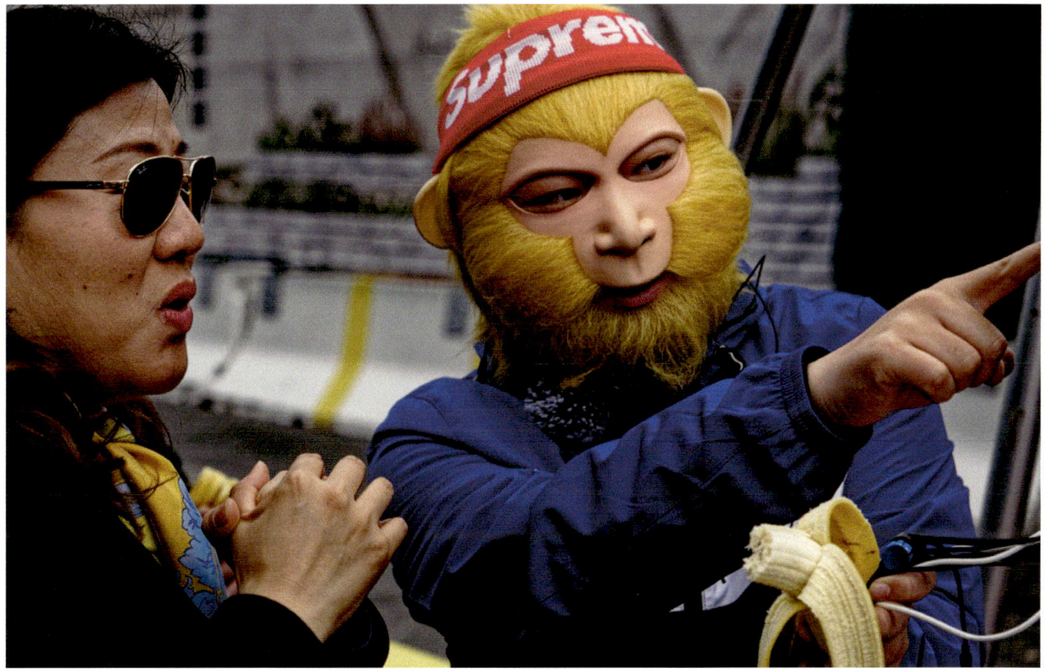

This courteous monkey directs a tourist to her destination. Not all encounters are helpful. Almost half of New Yorkers polled reported having unpleasant experiences with costumed characters and other street performers. (Hudson Yards.)

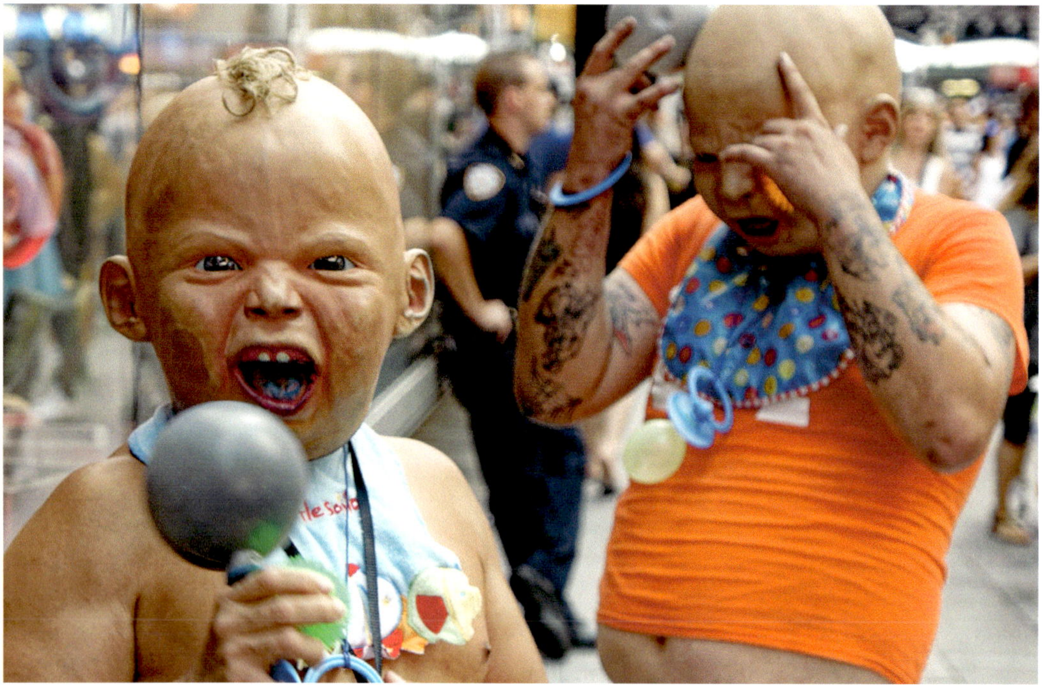

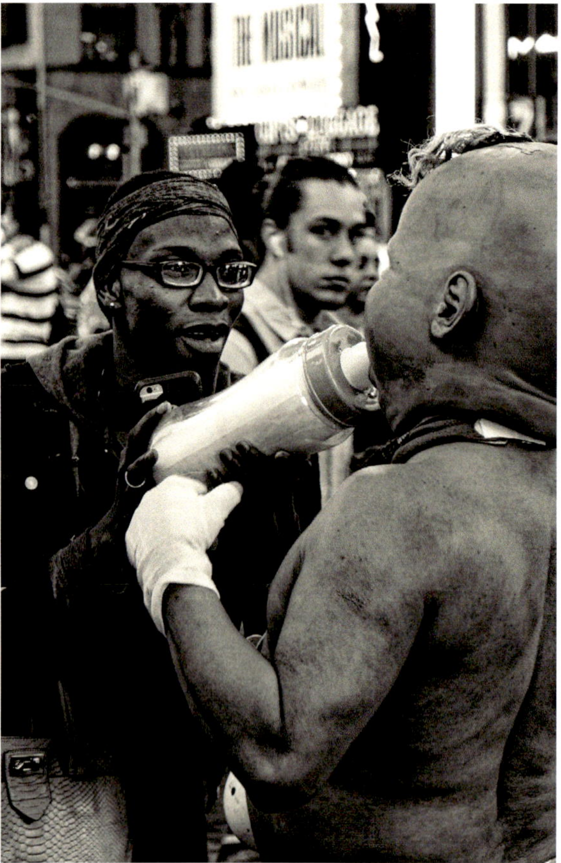

Above: Like the fake monks, costumed characters often make unwanted physical contact with pedestrians in an effort to extract payment for souvenir snapshots taken with them. To make matters worse, their behavior obstructs New Yorkers as they rush to and from work. (Times Square.)

Left: To manage the bottlenecking of street performers, tourists, and New Yorkers, specific areas have been set aside. "Designated Activity Zones," marked in blue, are for performers. "Chill Zones" are for relaxation and "Express Lanes" are for unimpeded pedestrian flow. (Times Square.)

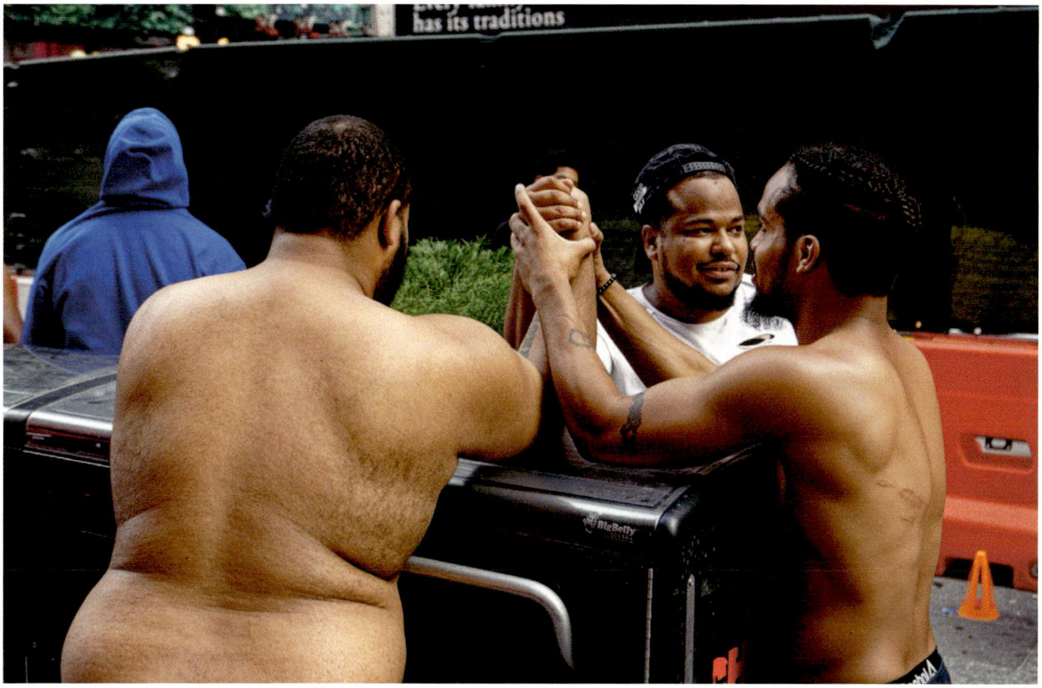

Above: Man-Babies are wearing nothing more than diapers and a bib. Shirtless friends are arm wrestling on a hot, humid day. These are among the quirky sights that go unchallenged, unlike performers whose attire, or lack thereof, has stirred controversy. (Broadway.)

Right: While it is generally acceptable for men to be topless, it is not the case for women, even though New York State's highest court ruled it to be legal in 1992. (Times Square.)

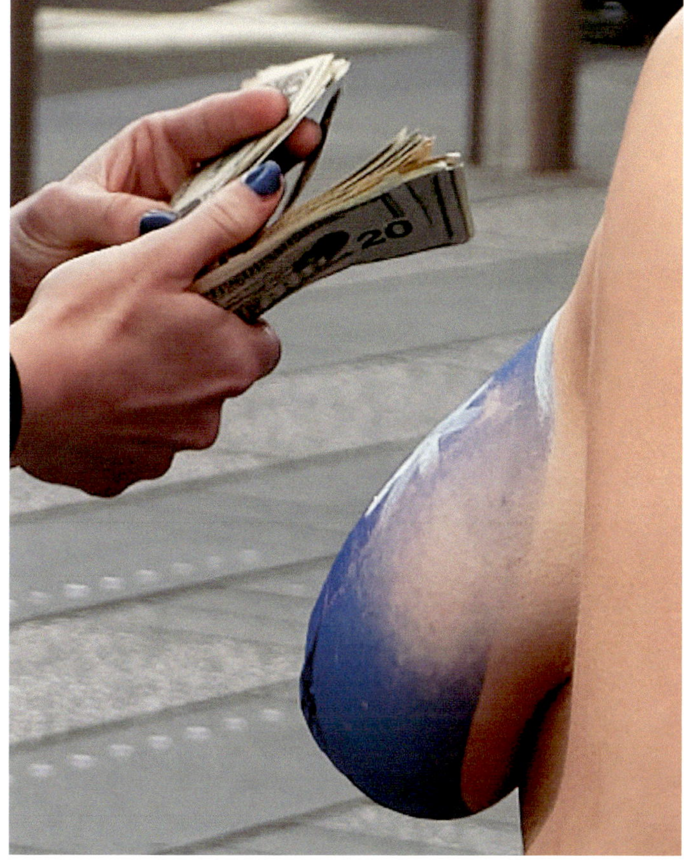

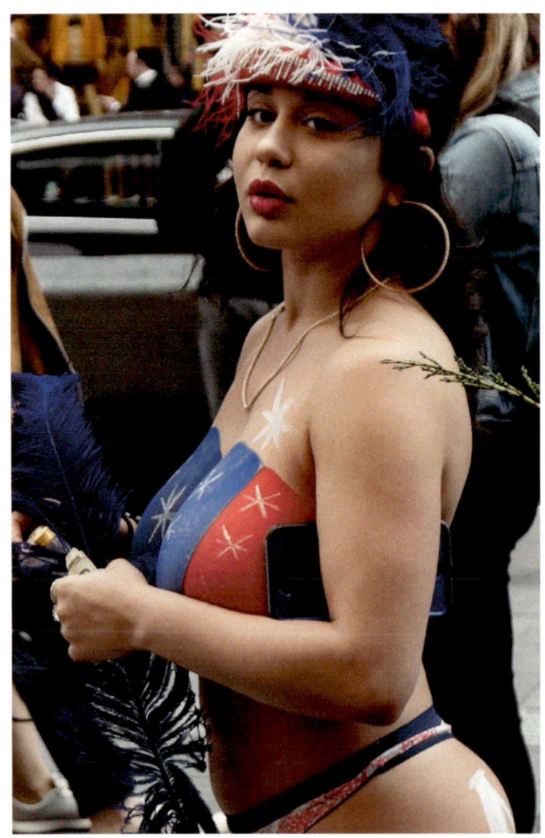

The *desnudas* (Spanish for nude) are mostly young Latinas adorned with feathers on their heads, wedge heels on their feet, and in between, just a thong and body paint. (Times Square.)

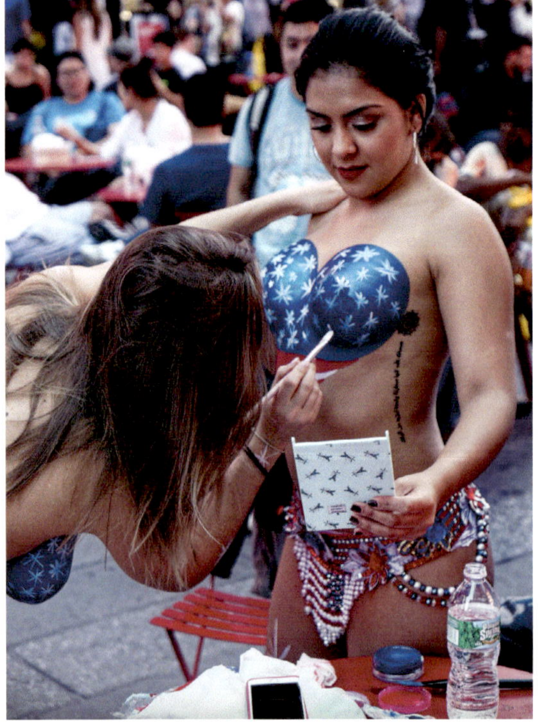

The *desnudas* call to mind the female topless performers at Las Vegas shows and Brazil's Carnaval or the Bourbon Street ritual of exposing breasts in exchange for Mardi Gras beads. The difference is that, in New York City, their appearance on the street is a daily event during the warmer seasons. (Times Square.)

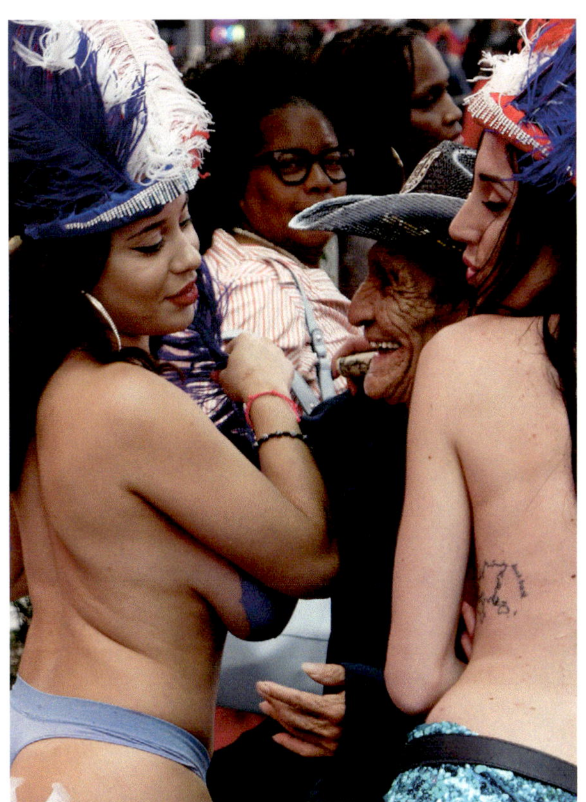

Opponents argue that the *desnudas* violate public decency, make families uncomfortable, can be as aggressive as fake monks and costumed characters, and deter tourism. (Times Square.)

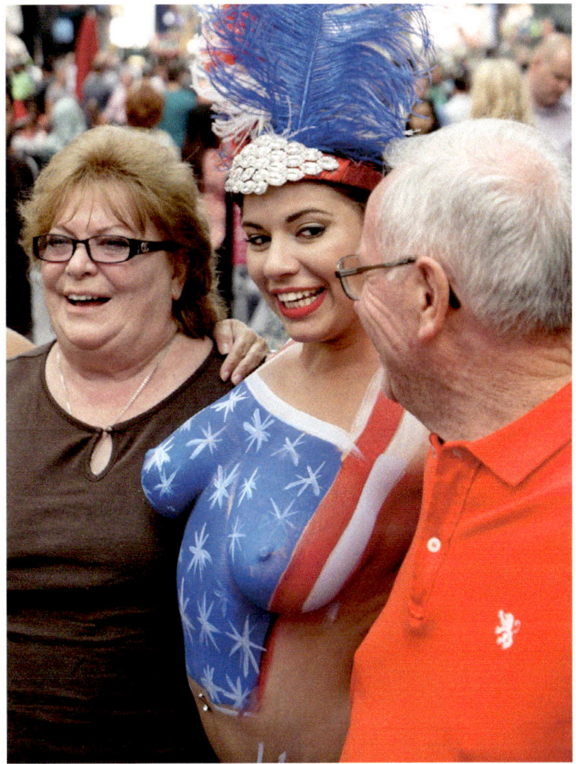

Supporters argue that these painted entertainers promote body art and personal freedom by liberating the female breast, reflecting what makes New York a special attraction for visitors. (Times Square.)

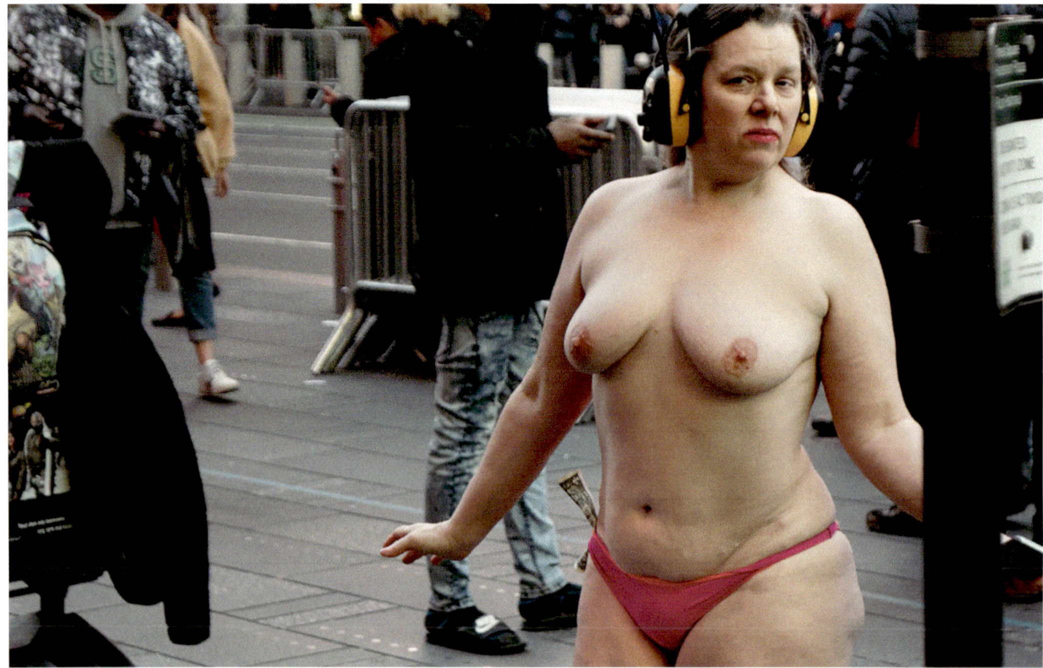

Occasionally, all attempts at creating art are set aside; the skin remains untouched by paint, and a radio headset takes the place of feathers. (Times Square.)

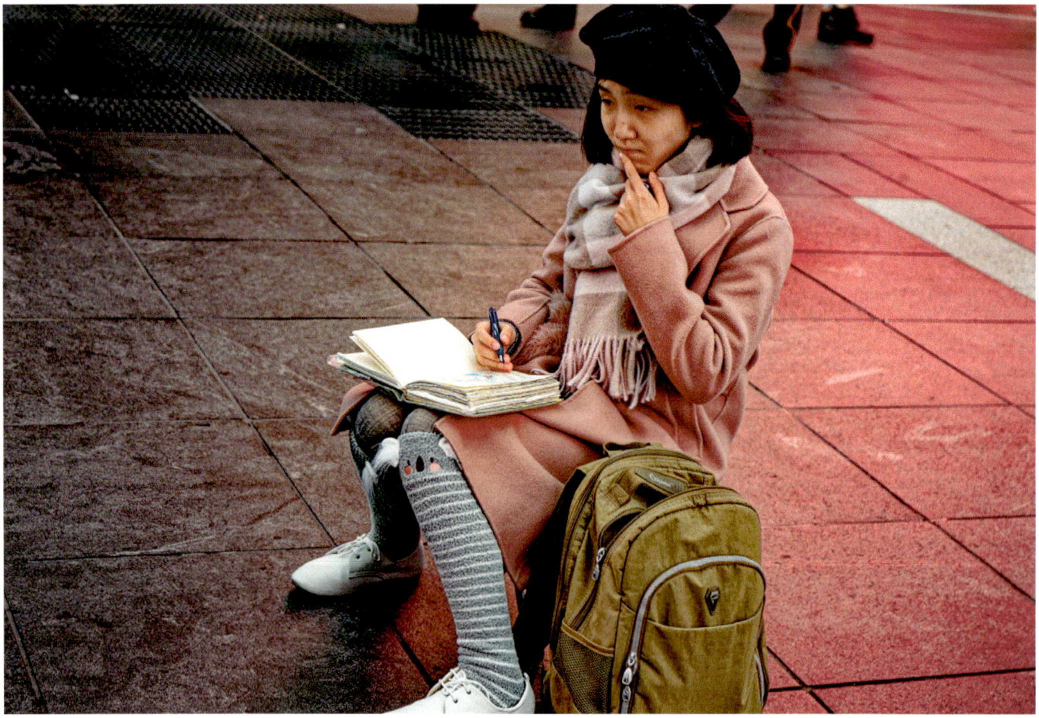

New York is a confounding torrent of complexities, dangers, absurdities, eccentricities, and contradictions. The mélange gives the city its unique urban personality. (Times Square.)

2
Signs of the Times

"Ey! I'm wawkin' heah!" shouts Ratso Rizzo in *Midnight Cowboy*'s taxi scene. When provoked, that old-time New York aggression explodes out of me too. There was that time when a fake monk "gifted" me with a shiny, gold amulet card while demanding money. I scolded him. He got nasty. I took his picture. He hit my camera and then I … well, it got ugly real fast. I kept the card. It says, "Lifetime Peace."

I used to be worse, and so was New York. For me, it was a grim, overcast world of "Noo Yawk" accents, graffiti, litter, broken glass, dog excrement, and an infinity of discarded pull tabs from beer and soda cans. I was burglarized, robbed, and threatened. I still have an injury from being assaulted.

Nowadays, I rarely hear anyone who sounds like Al Pacino or Cyndi Lauper. The population is larger and more diverse, but the streets are cleaner with reduced racial tensions. Fiscally, the city is more stable even after the dual punches of the Great Recession and the pandemic. Crime has been decreasing, attributed (in part) to a larger police force and stricter gun laws.

Times Square is where the transformation really hits home. The old version, seen in the 1971 movie *The French Connection*, was an urban jungle of pornography theaters, cheap dilapidated hotels, drugs, alcoholism, prostitution, con games, and homeless people. It was a blighted neighborhood that pedestrians, especially women, avoided.

Now it is safe for public expression. News, opinions, and advertisements are broadcast by television networks and big-name brands from the skyscrapers above. On the streets below, protestors project their own agendas as a counterbalance, hoping that corporate media will report and magnify their causes. It was liberating to photograph people who welcomed my camera. I like seeing hands raised for displaying signs, rather than in surrender to muggers.

Private thoughts are also shared anonymously or by a lone individual. Universal sentiments, like hopes and fears, can resonate with almost anyone, regardless of their views about the government or the culture wars. Sometimes, random juxtapositions of signage transmit unintended messages, as if the city is speaking through its own spirit. The tendency to perceive meaningful connections between unrelated things where none actually exist is a psychological phenomenon. These manifestations are good with art, music, and poetry and bad with racism, conspiracy theories, and seeing the Virgin Mary on a grilled cheese sandwich. Perhaps this chapter's greater number of stark, gritty, black and white photographs is my way of connecting the "new" New York with the old one I remember.

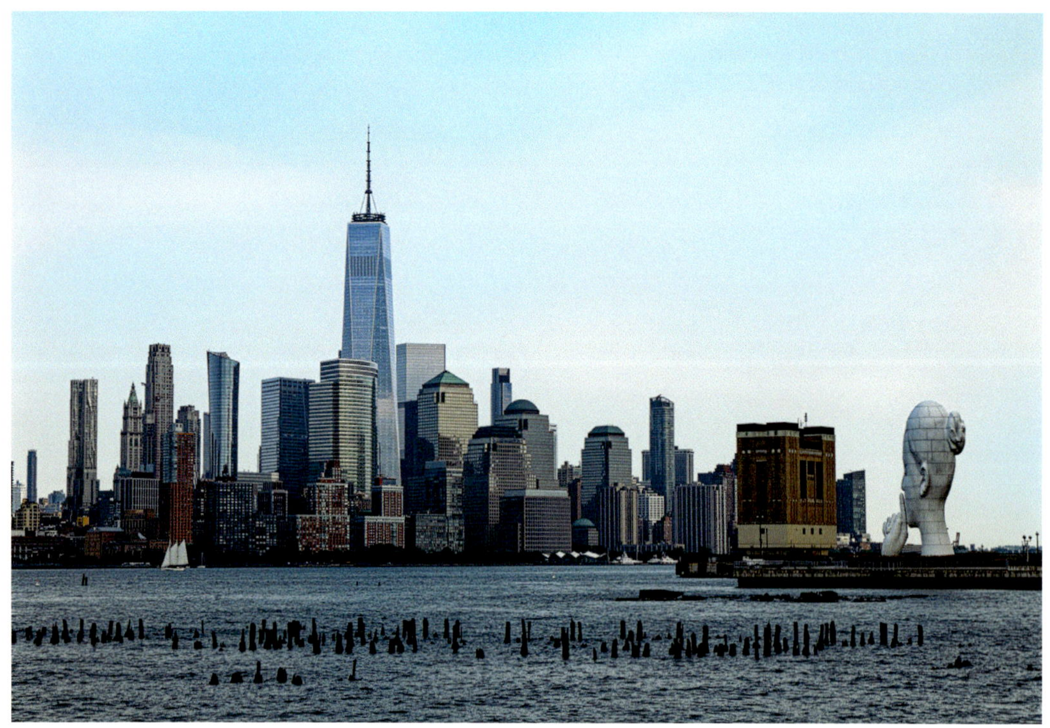

Try as she might, the *Water's Soul* sculpture (on the right) is never going to shush New York City. (Hudson River Waterfront Walkway, New Jersey.)

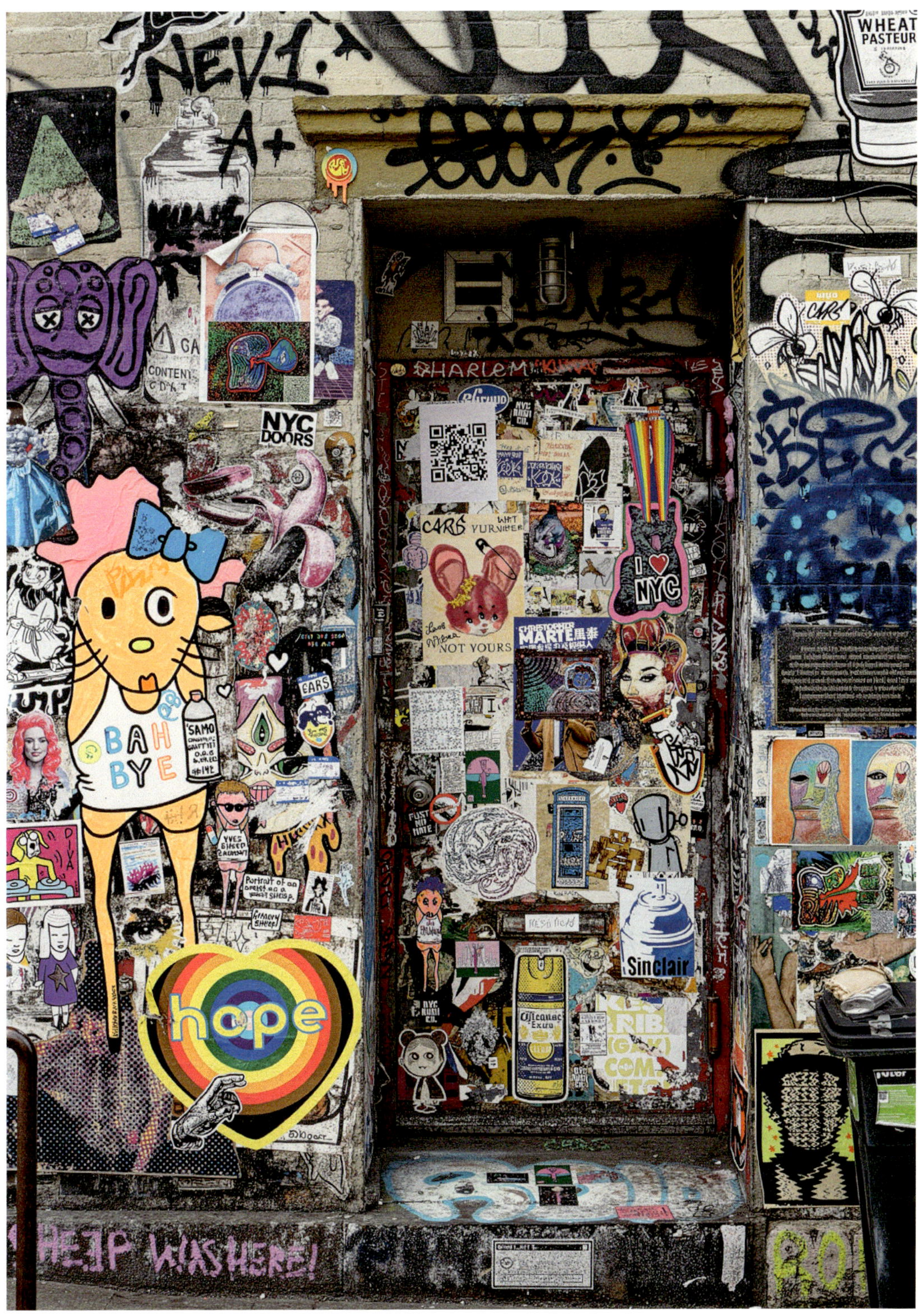

New Yorkers are known for being outspoken. They are not afraid to say what they think. It ranges from the serious to the humorous. (NoHo District, 57 Great Jones Street.)

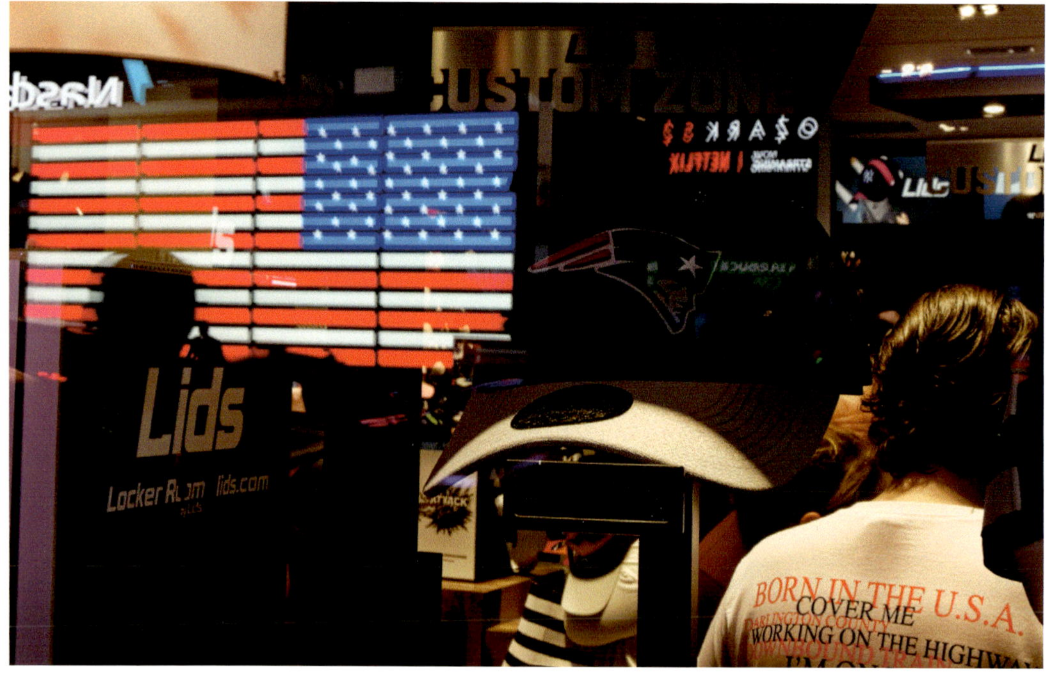

The First Amendment right to free speech is zealously exercised in the Big Apple. Times Square, a focal point of the city, serves as a convenient vocal point as well. (Times Square.)

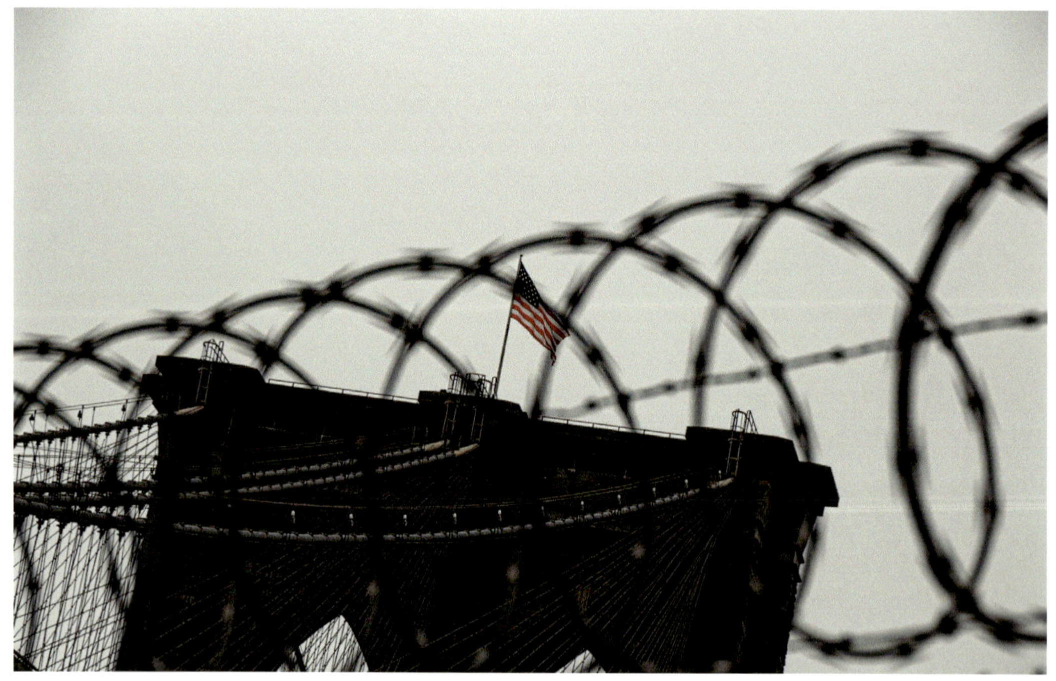

There have always been bouts of political and cultural upheaval. But it seems that, ever since the 9/11 attacks on the World Trade Center, the city and the nation have been struggling with existential crises. (Brooklyn Bridge.)

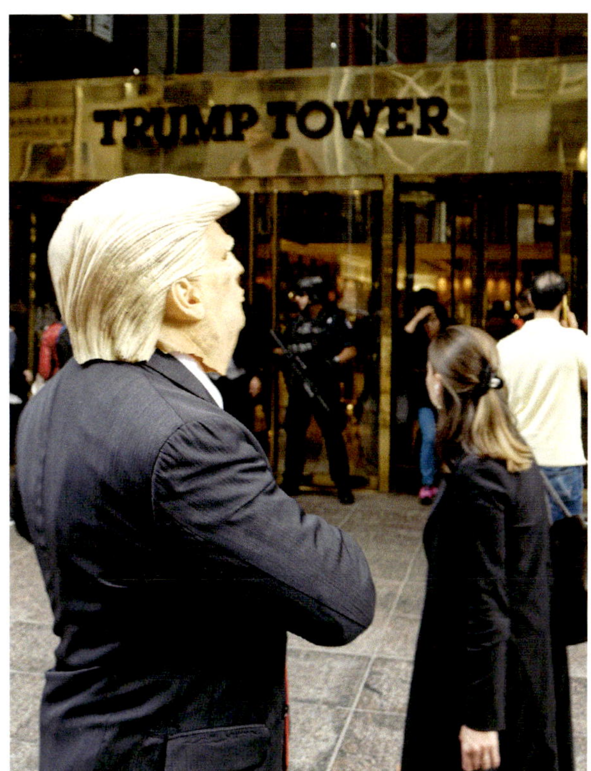

The political rancor was exacerbated with the rise of Donald Trump. Even with his high-profile presence in Manhattan dating back to the 1970s, few would have thought Trump's "Make America Great" movement would have mustered any traction in a historically liberal city. (725 5th Avenue.)

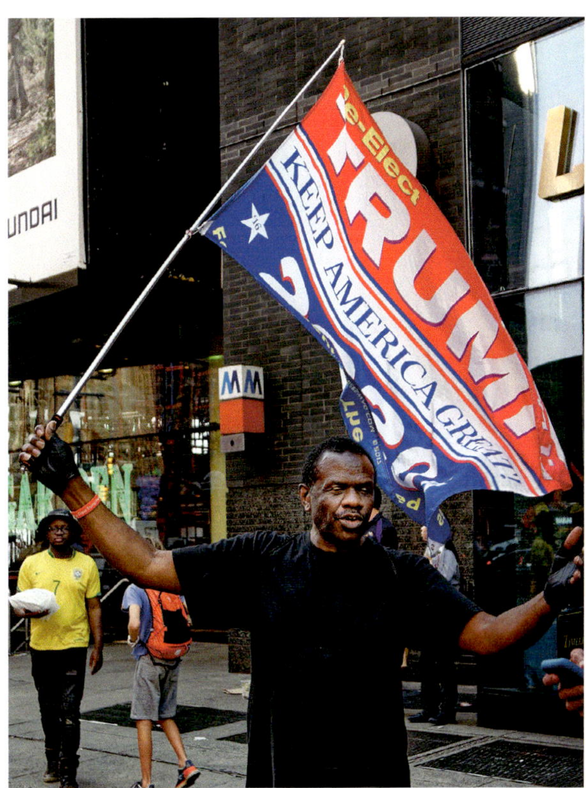

Voting blocs presumed to be monolithic were starting to change. Signs of this shift were conspicuously showing up on the street. (714 7th Avenue.)

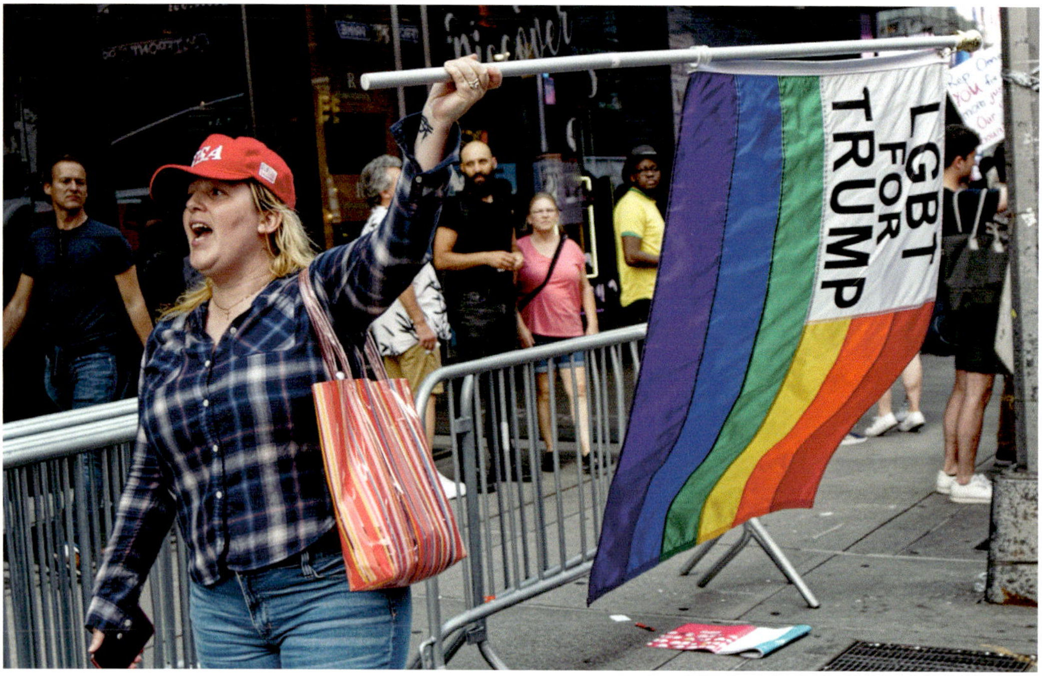

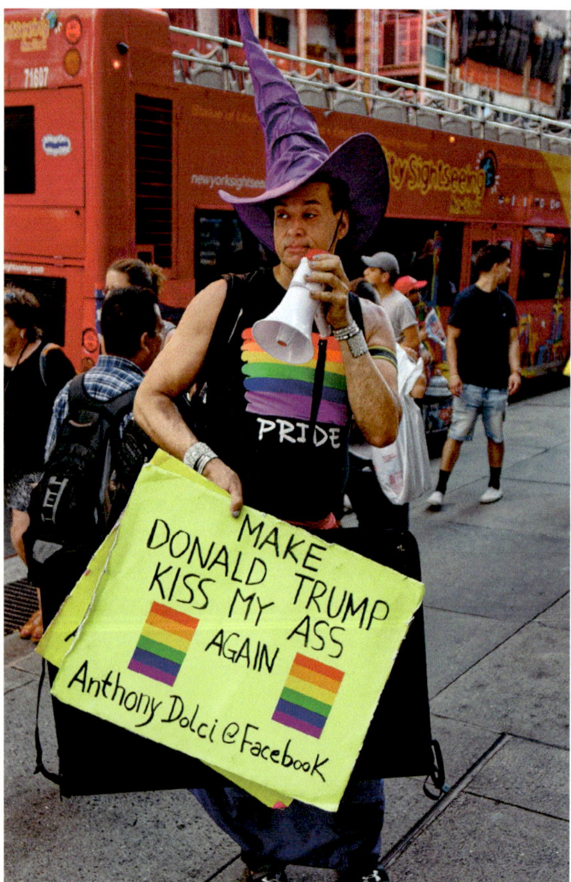

Above: New, non-traditional alliances were being formed. The old adage was ringing true that "politics makes strange bedfellows." (714 7th Avenue.)

Left: The divisiveness continued to deepen within these groups, and opposition was voiced with typical New York flair and bluntness. (7th Avenue at West 48th Street.)

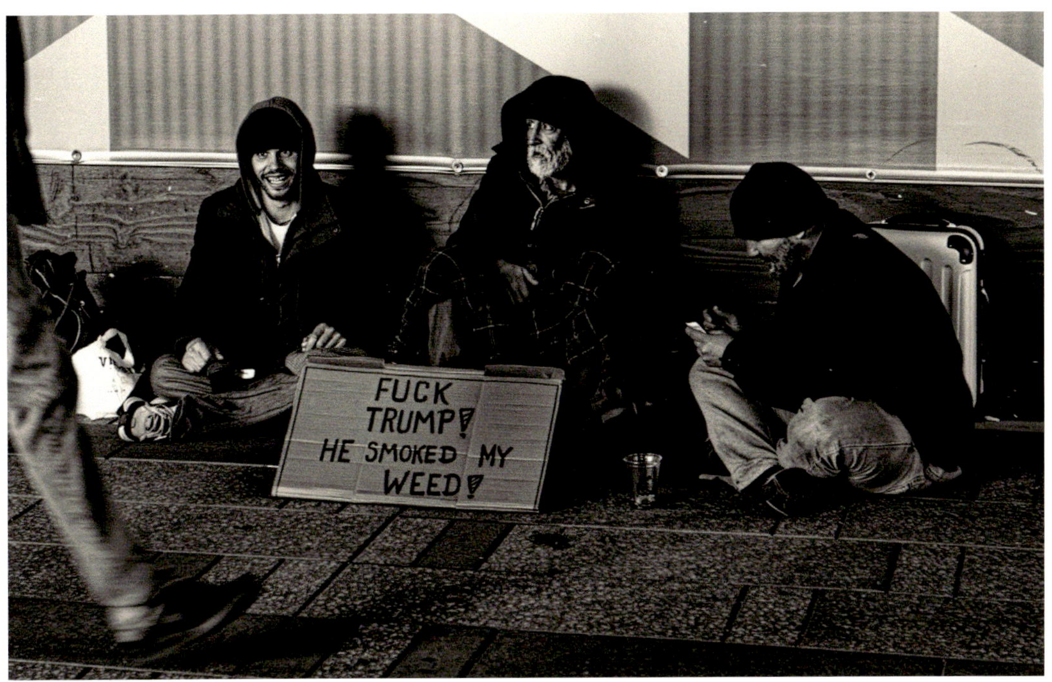

Those on the periphery of society, accustomed to being ignored by passersby, joined the fray as well by calling attention in colorfully creative ways. (Times Square.)

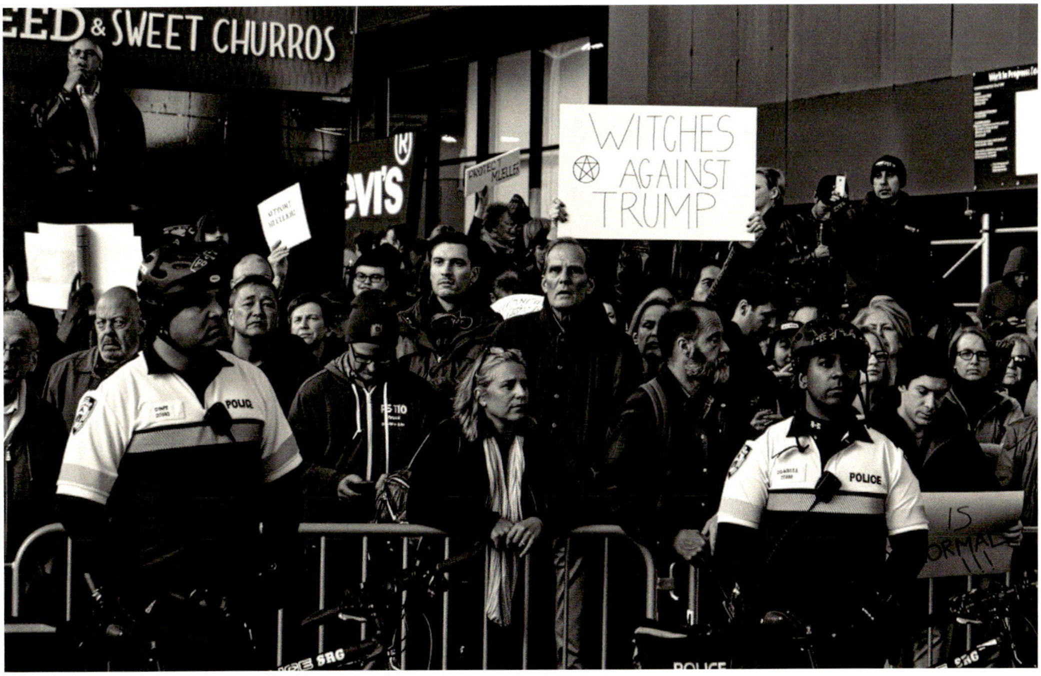

This collective outrage came to a head in "the crossroads of the world." It was spellbinding to see the variety of special interest groups drawn there. (Times Square.)

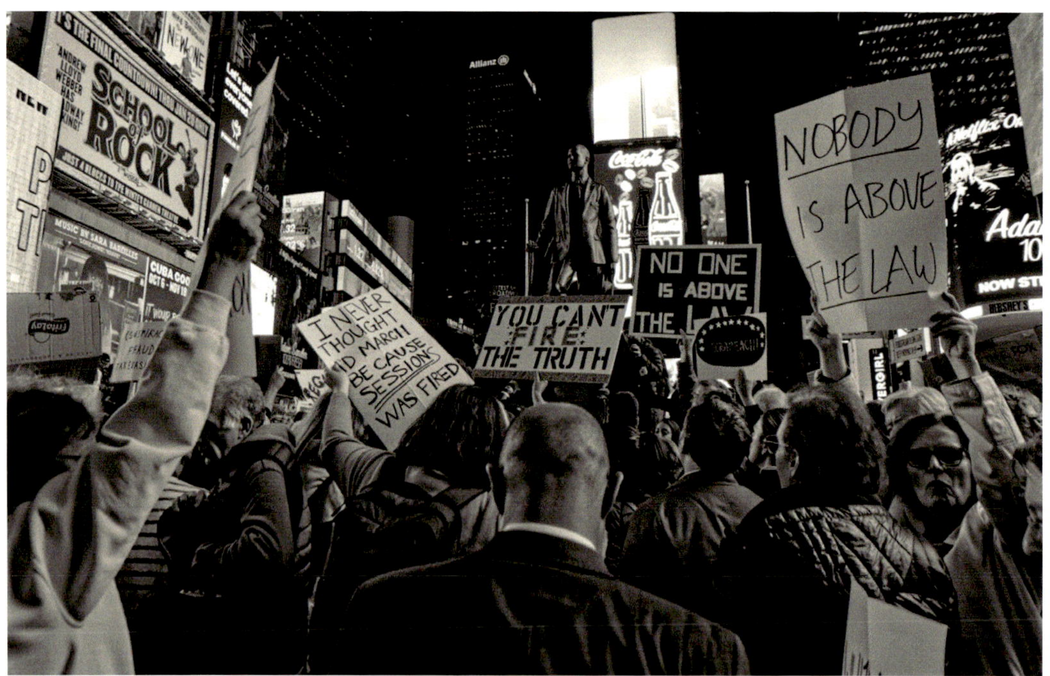

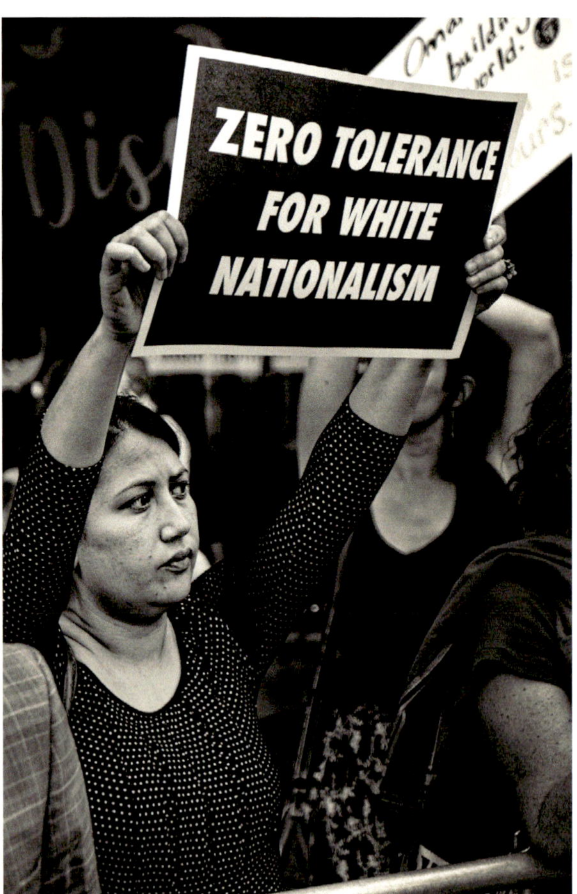

Above: It can also be a jarring experience considering it is where the famous New Year's Eve ball is dropped. The celebration is one of the few unifying events enjoyed throughout the nation and abroad. (Times Square.)

Left: The area is ideal for amplifying a message. It is easy to get there by foot, subway, or bus, and the intersection provides exposure to both locals and international tourists. More importantly, numerous major news media organizations have offices in or near the neighborhood. (Times Square.)

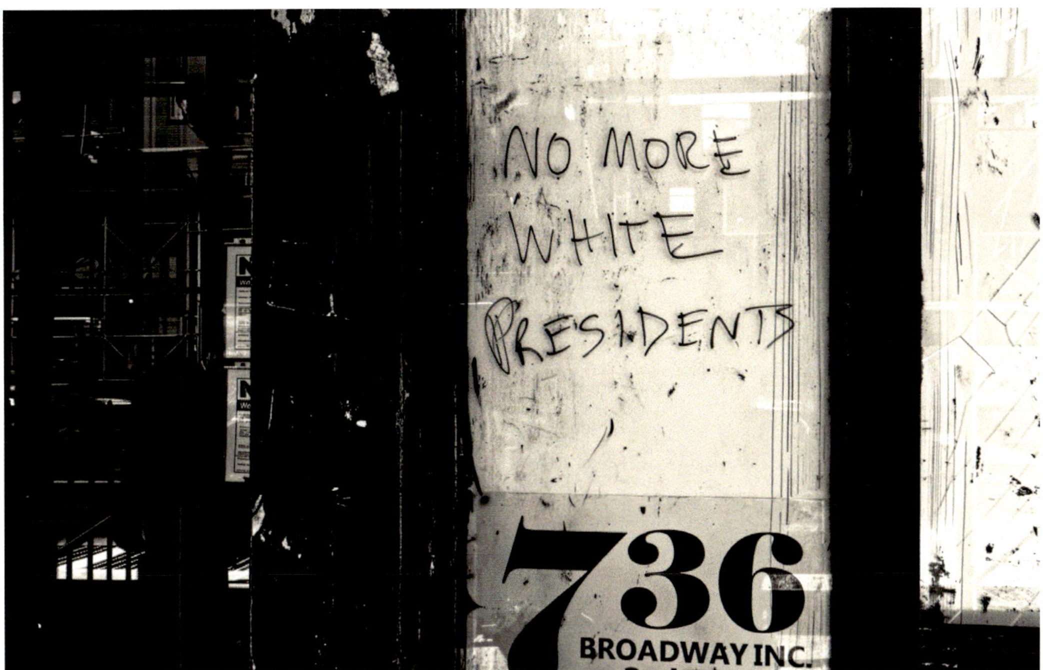

Free speech is by no means limited to that section of midtown Manhattan. Sometimes opinions sprout out elsewhere and in unexpected places like a closed downtown storefront near New York University. (Greenwich Village.)

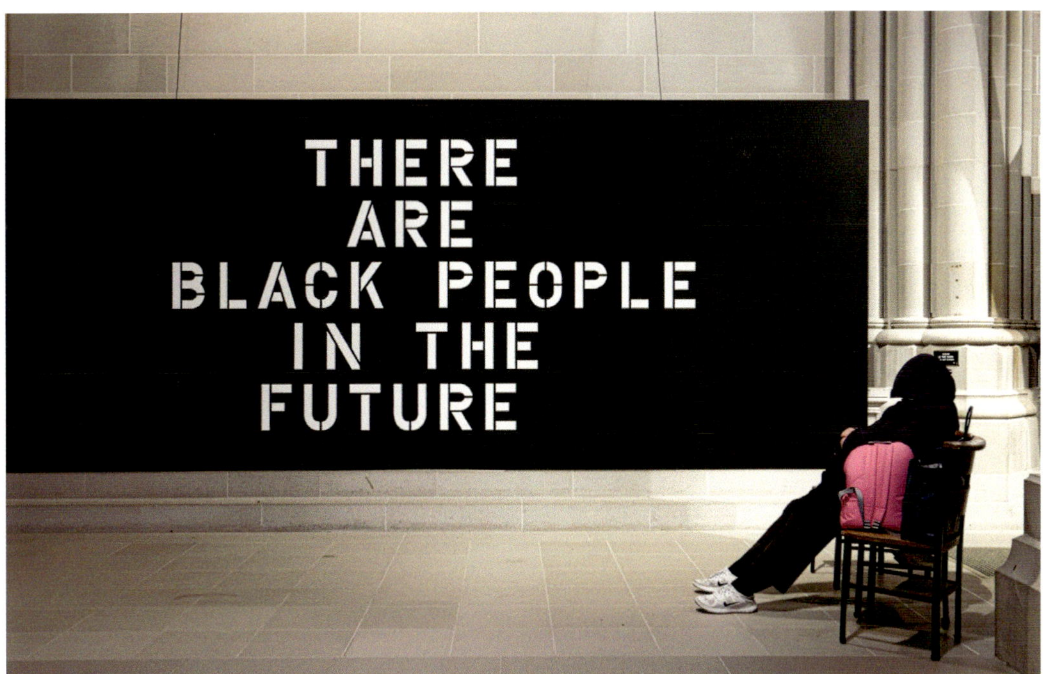

Statements may even get showcased in a house of worship in the Upper West Side near Columbia University. (The Cathedral Church of Saint John the Divine.)

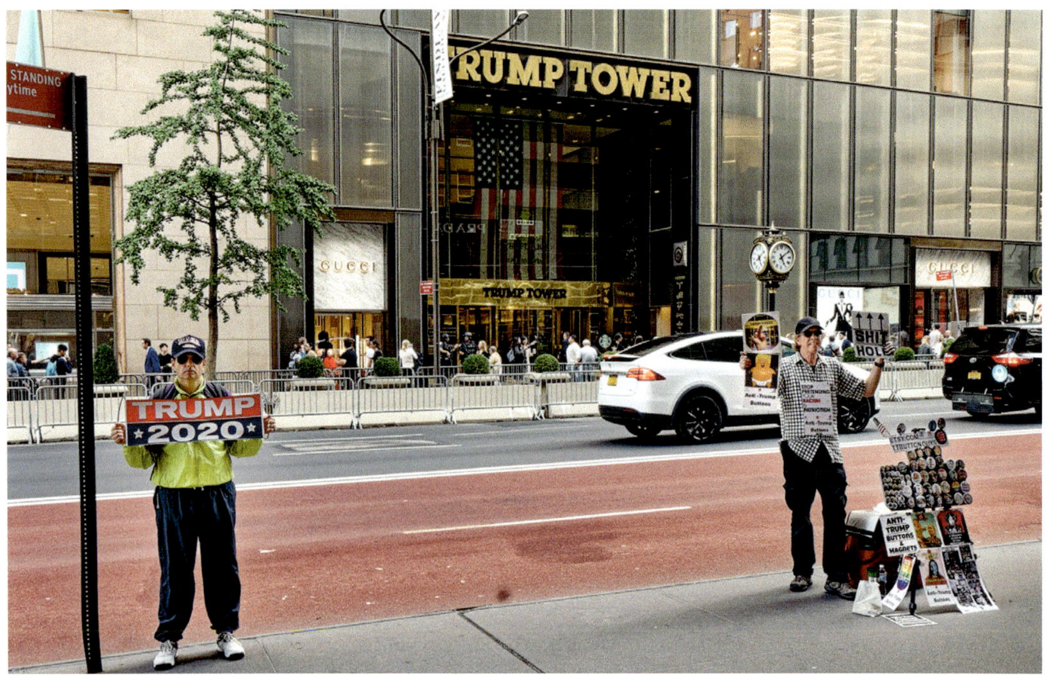

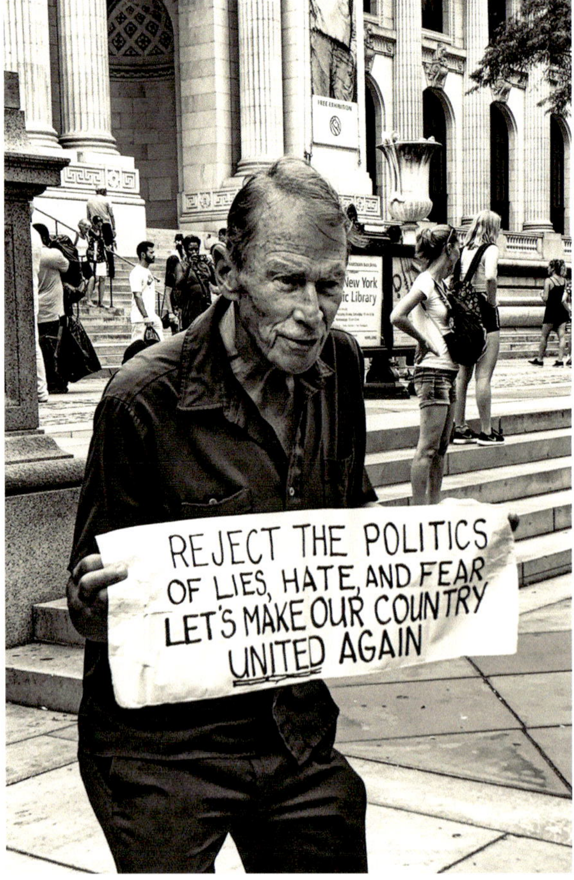

Above: In any case, wherever the location, the polarization was becoming more starkly displayed and, most notably, right in front of Trump Tower. (730 5th Avenue.)

Left: Every now and then, a small sign of encouragement and hope fights through the increasingly negative clamor. (New York Public Library, 5th Avenue.)

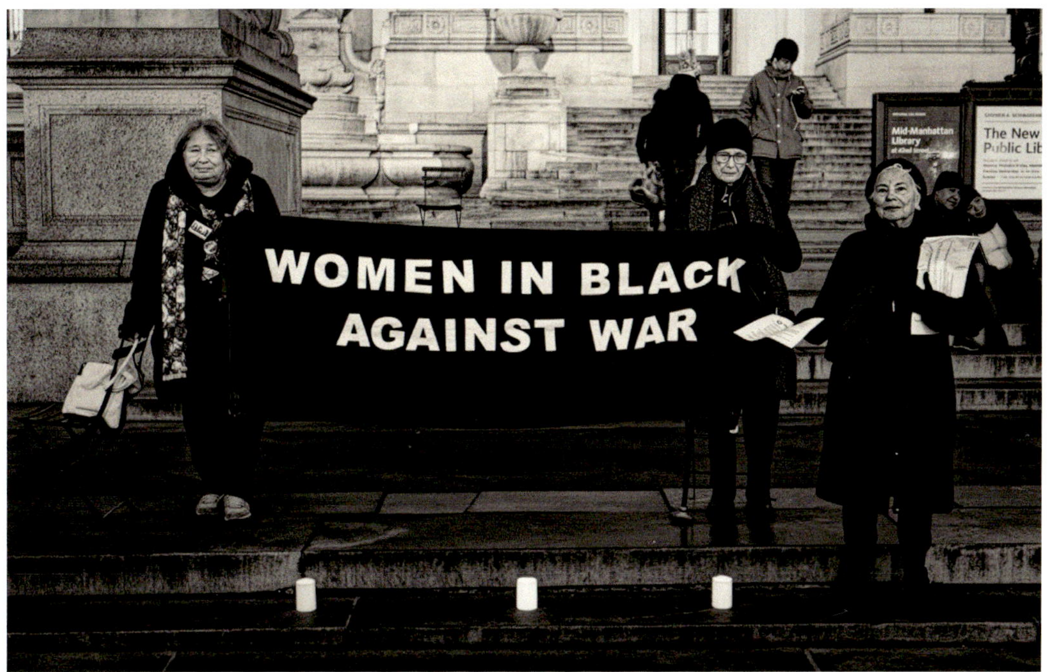

The turmoil, though, is much more widespread and complicated than the partisan quarrels erupting across the country. (New York Public Library, 5th Avenue.)

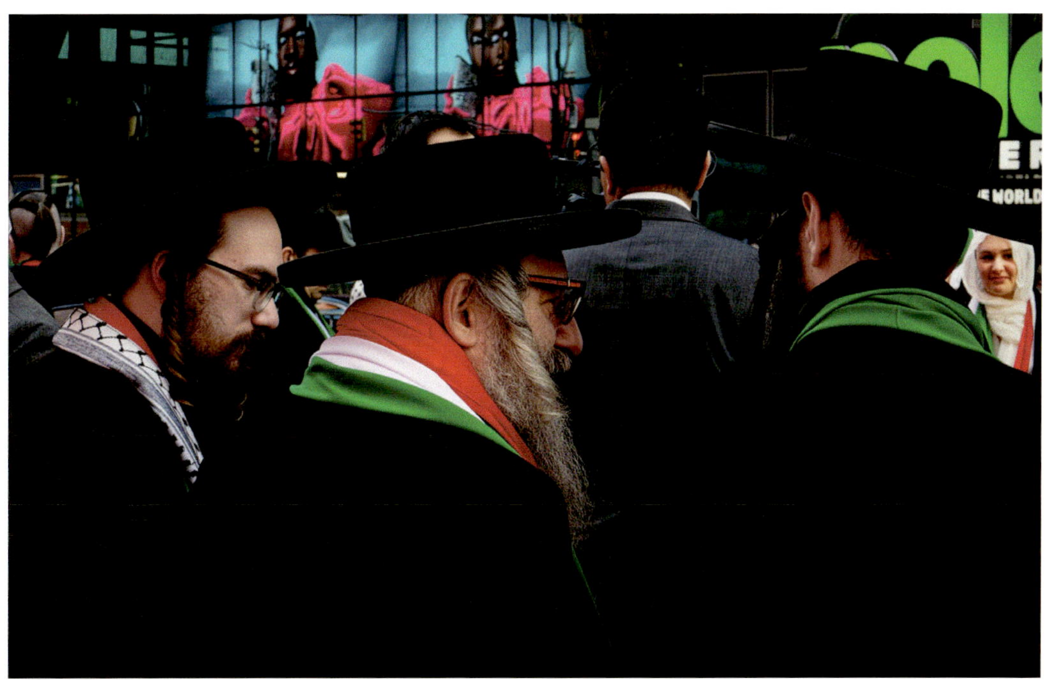

Unpredictable events in hotspots around the world have a way of making a dramatic impact on the city too. (Times Square.)

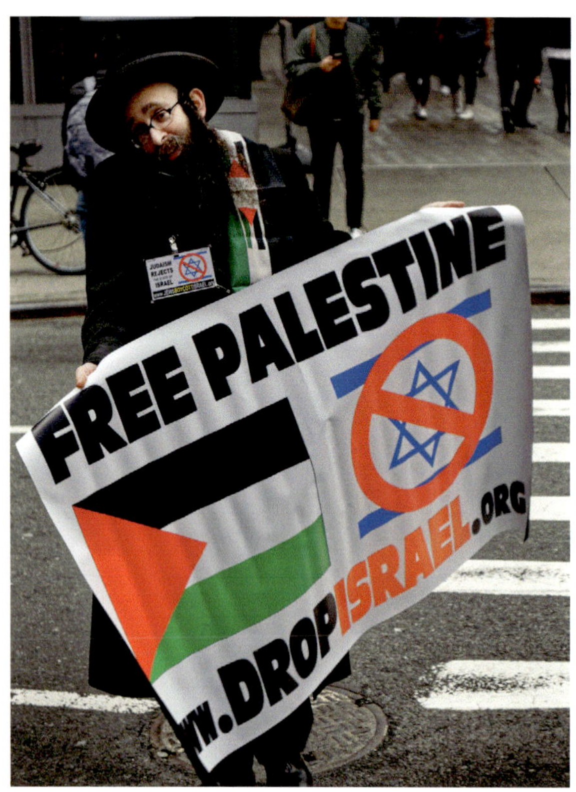

The reaction here can be unpredictable as well, and its repercussions resonate far beyond the confines of Times Square. (7th Avenue.)

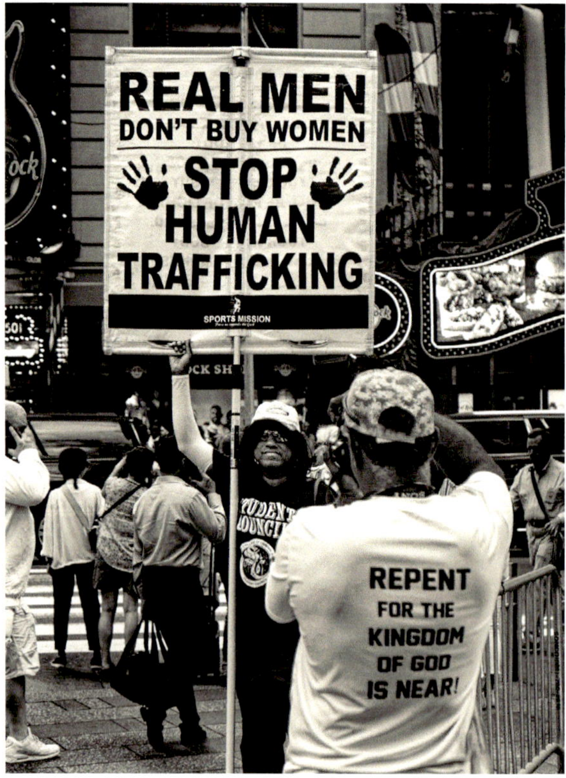

Global issues, such as human rights violations, are a frequent catalyst for protest. The serious nature of the messaging becomes surreal against the backdrop of theaters and other entertainment venues. (Times Square.)

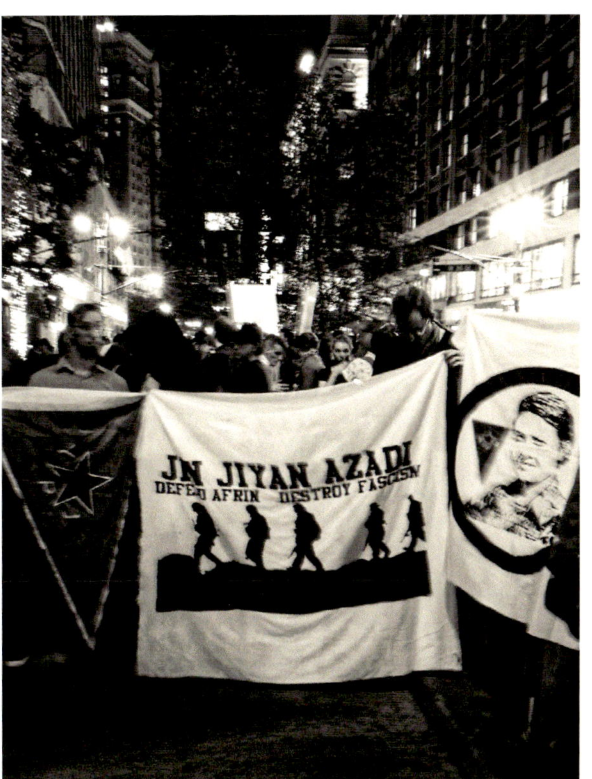

Specific conflicts also come under fire. "Jin, Jiyan, Azadi," which is Kurdish for "Woman, Life, Freedom," calls attention to the repression of women's rights by Iran's "morality police." (Broadway.)

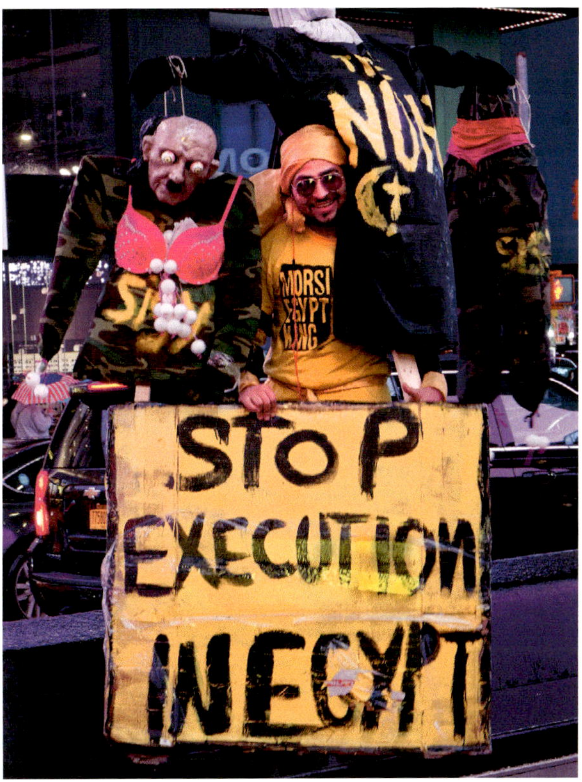

The city's sizable foreign-born population is among the highest in America. With over 200 nationalities represented, it is not unusual for a home country's controversies to come under scrutiny from the audience at the world's biggest stage. (Times Square.)

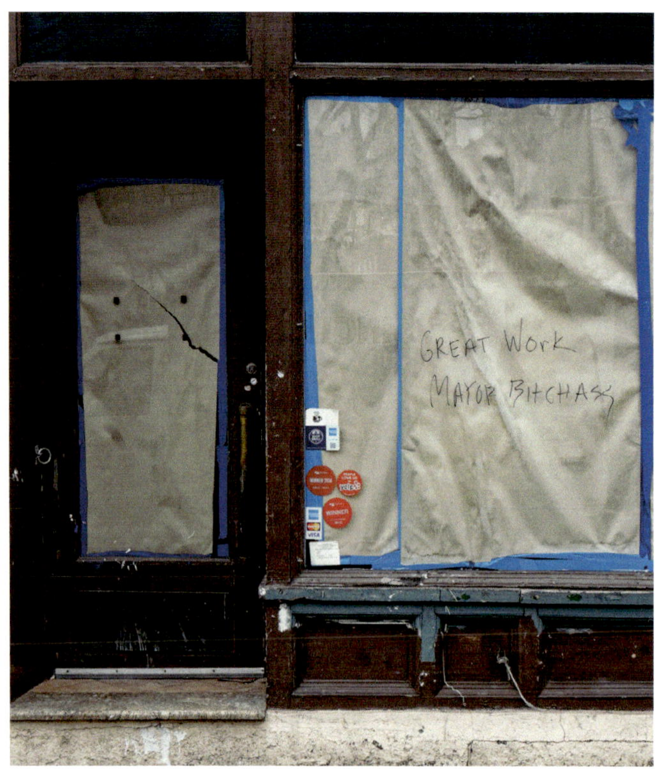

As weighty as these international issues are, personal grievances on a more local scale by average New Yorkers find their place in public discourse. (Greenwich Avenue, Greenwich Village.)

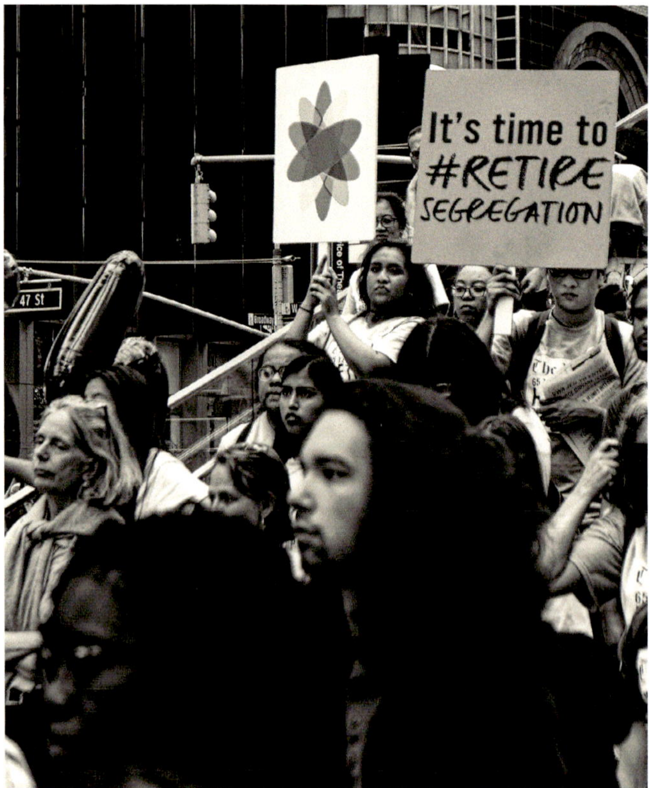

Here, a mostly younger crowd gathers on the anniversary of the 1954 U.S. Supreme Court ruling that racial segregation in public schools is unconstitutional. The demonstrators demand greater integration and equity in the city's public school system. (Times Square, West 47th Street.)

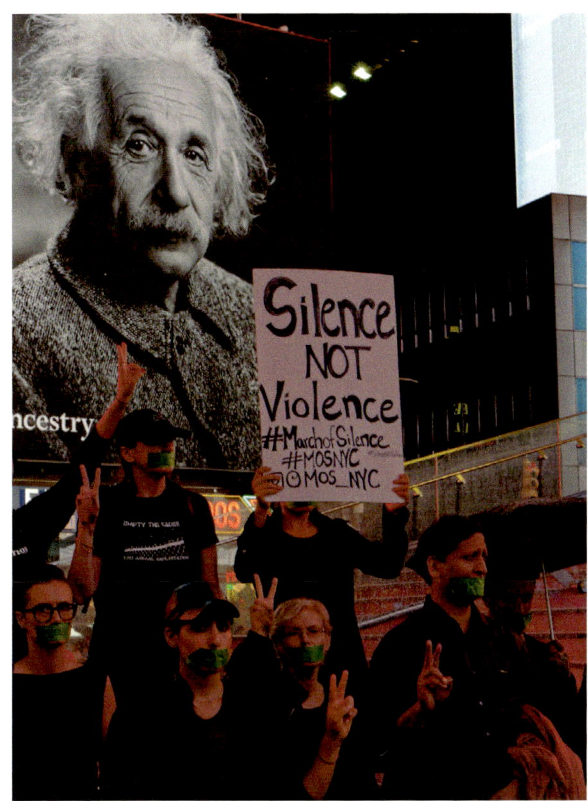

Even non-human creatures who are unable to speak for themselves can count on animal liberation activists to take to the streets and raise awareness on their behalf. (Times Square.)

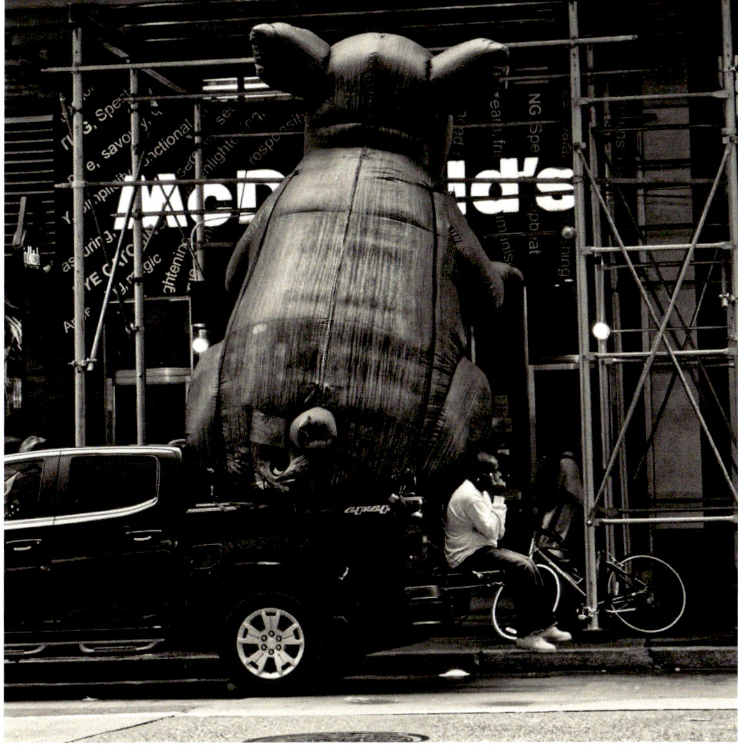

For this particular animal, silence is not an issue by virtue of its size. If a business employs nonunion labor, "Scabby the Rat" is certain to show up and object. (6th Avenue at West 46th Street.)

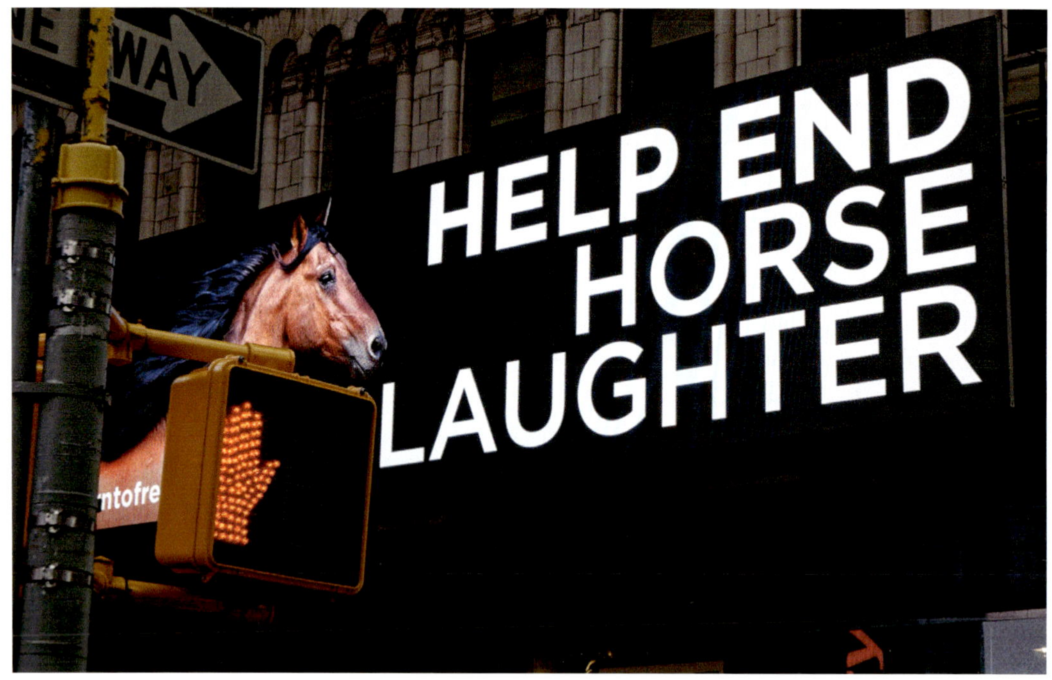

The semiotic clutter and chaos are so dense that they can momentarily overlap. A pedestrian's glance may get met with an unintended and perplexing message. (7th Avenue.)

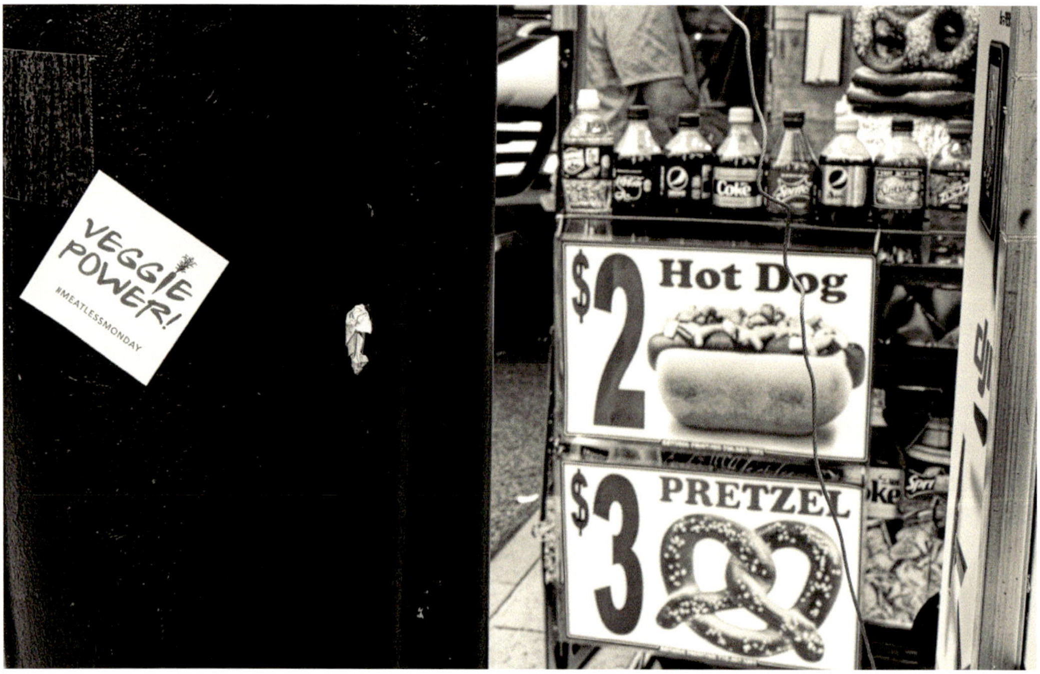

It is as if the city has a mind of its own, creating an ephemeral collage where the mere turn of a head reveals a serendipitous and ironic juxtaposition. (5th Avenue.)

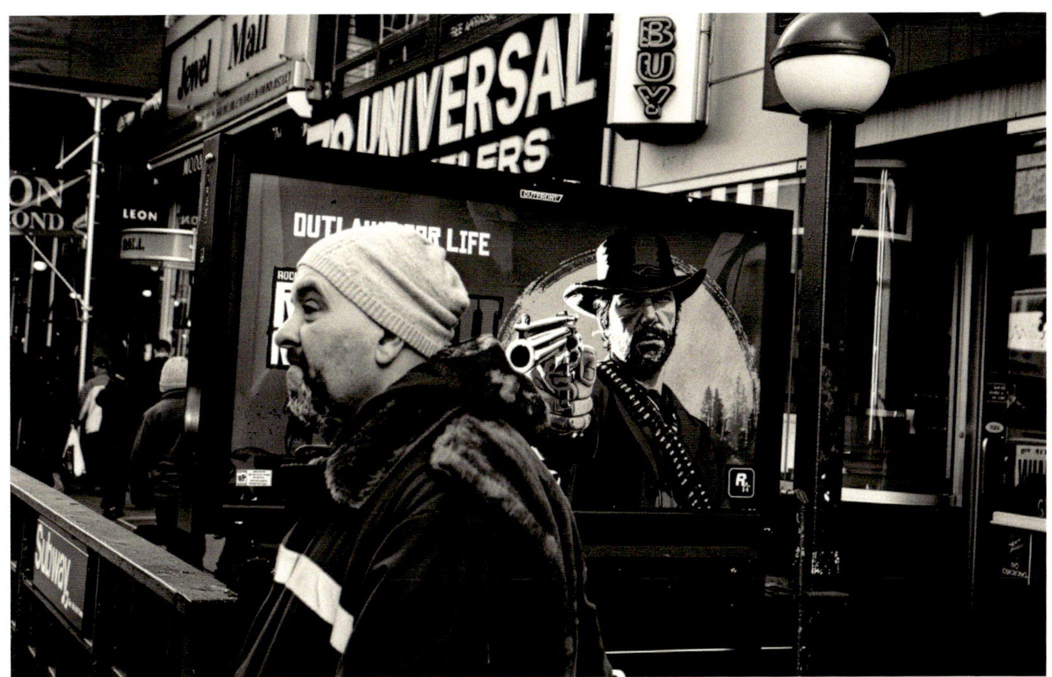

Above: Other times, the zeitgeist of the city chillingly and starkly points to the harsh realities of life and death in contemporary America. (6th Avenue at West 49th Street.)

Right: Manuel Oliver knows all too well. His seventeen-year-old son, Joaquin, was among the seventeen people killed in a mass shooting on Valentine's Day at Marjory Stoneman Douglas High School in Parkland, Florida. He was in New York bringing public attention to the scourge of gun violence. (Brooklyn Steel, 319 Frost Street.)

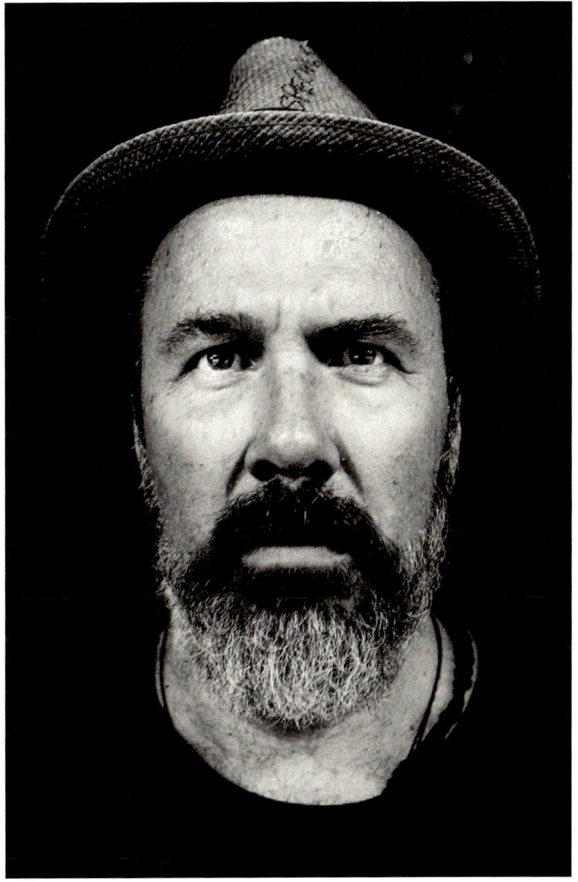

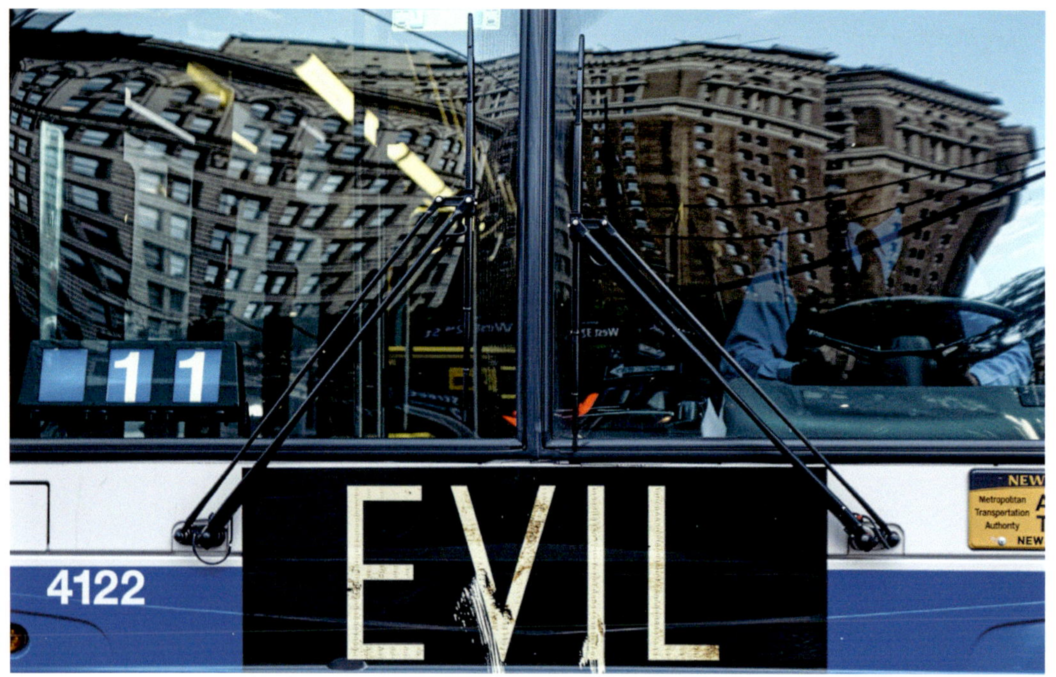

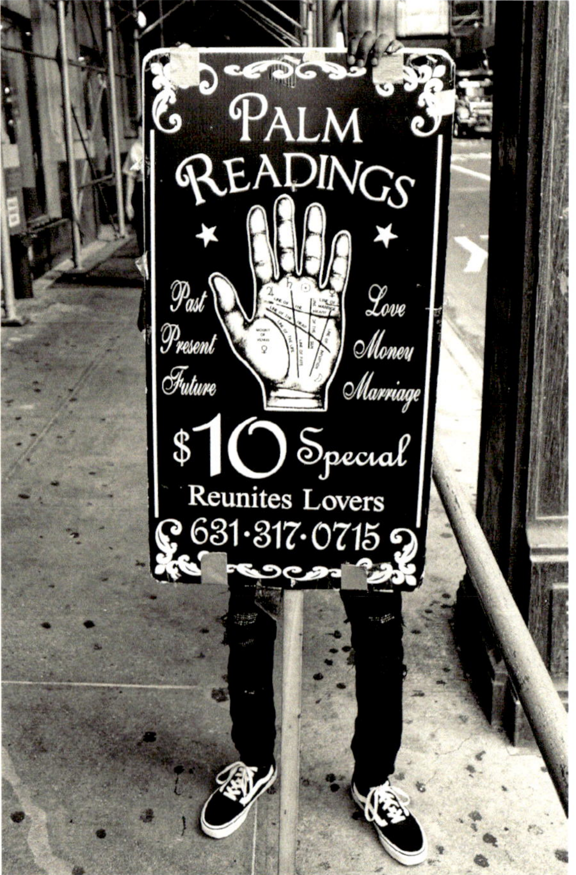

Above: Meanwhile, the living mourn the dead, legislators remain deadlocked about gun control, and intellectuals debate whether such a thing as evil is actually present in the world. (6th Avenue at West 32nd Street.)

Left: Scientists are skeptical about the supernatural, the paranormal, and other unexplainable psychic phenomena—realms into which the concept of evil bleeds. (8th Avenue.)

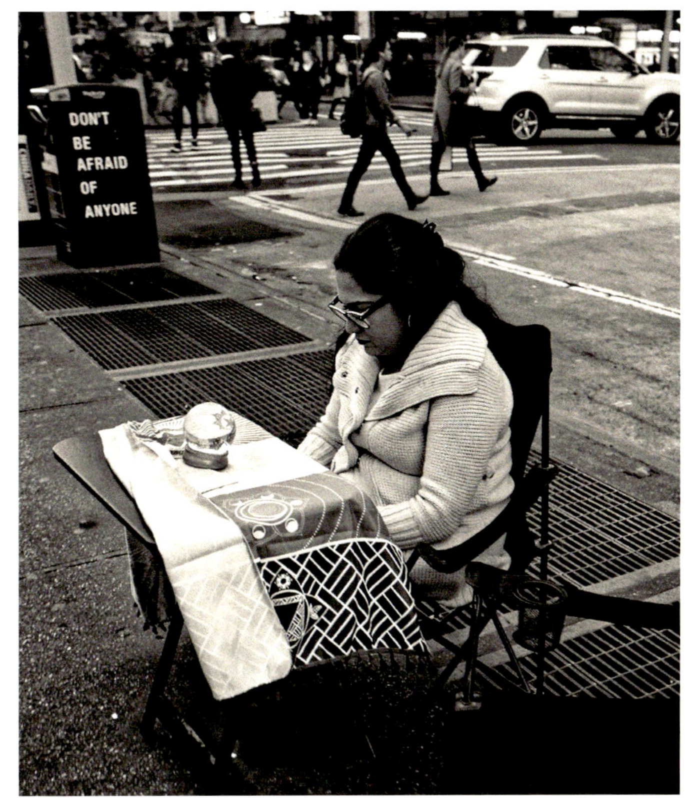

Right: However, for many people, fear of the unknown often gives rise to questions in the process of coping. This fear stems from a lack of control over events and fuels the search for understanding and meaning. (Broadway.)

Below: Although theologians have also grappled with the concept of evil, especially as it relates to the existence of a deity, there are believers who have no doubt about such matters and stand ready to proclaim their understanding of it. (Times Square, West 45th Street.)

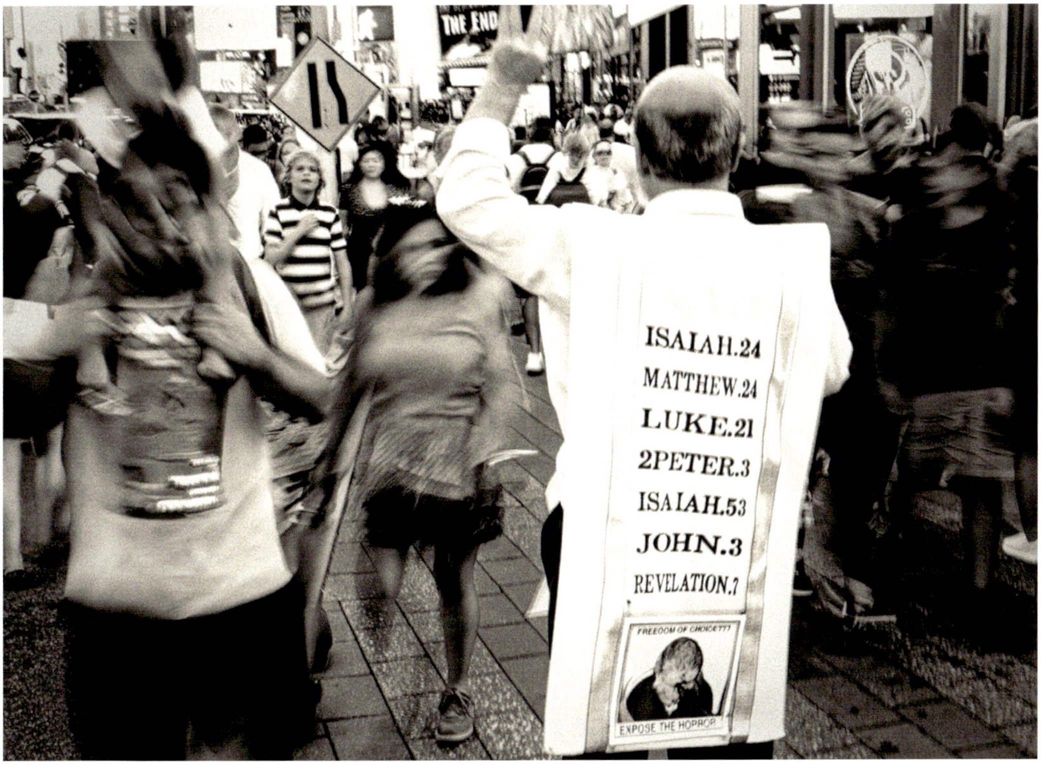

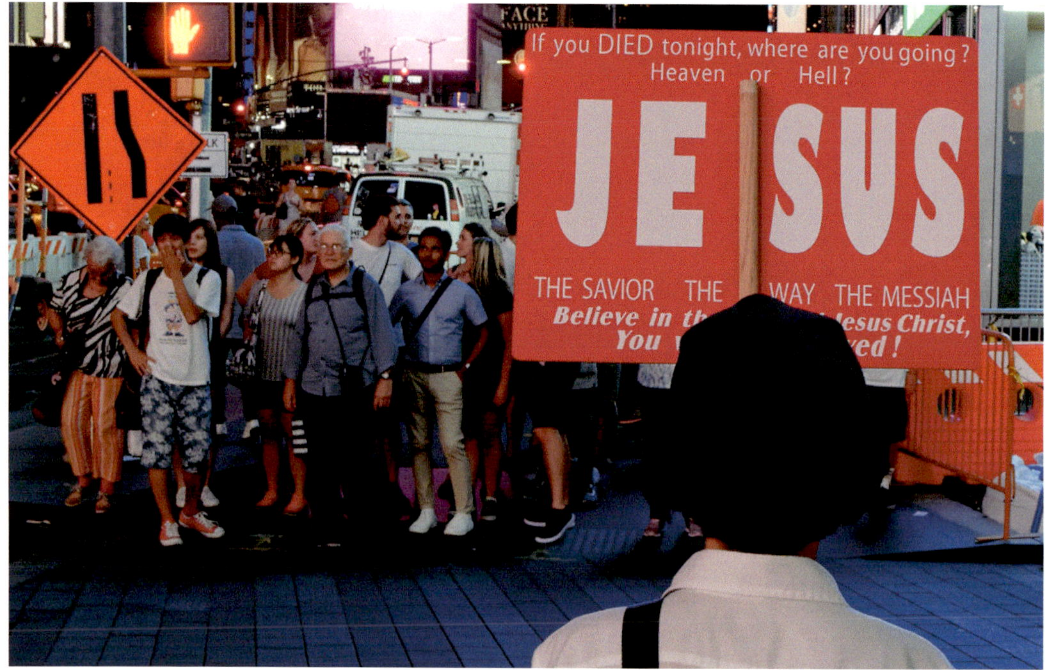

Some are eager to confront the public by posing questions about their mortality and exhorting them to follow what they believe is the only path. Freedom of religion is closely linked to the First Amendment, and this right is actively exercised alongside secular speech. (Times Square.)

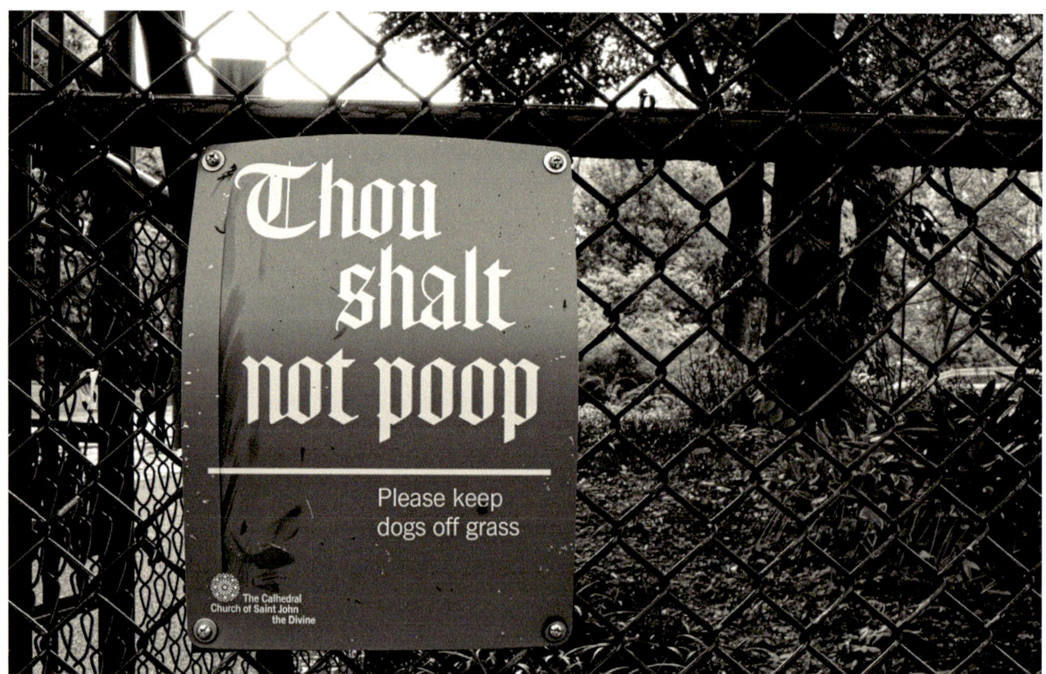

Other members of the faith community, in contrast, are more relaxed about how they connect with the public. (The Cathedral Church of Saint John the Divine.)

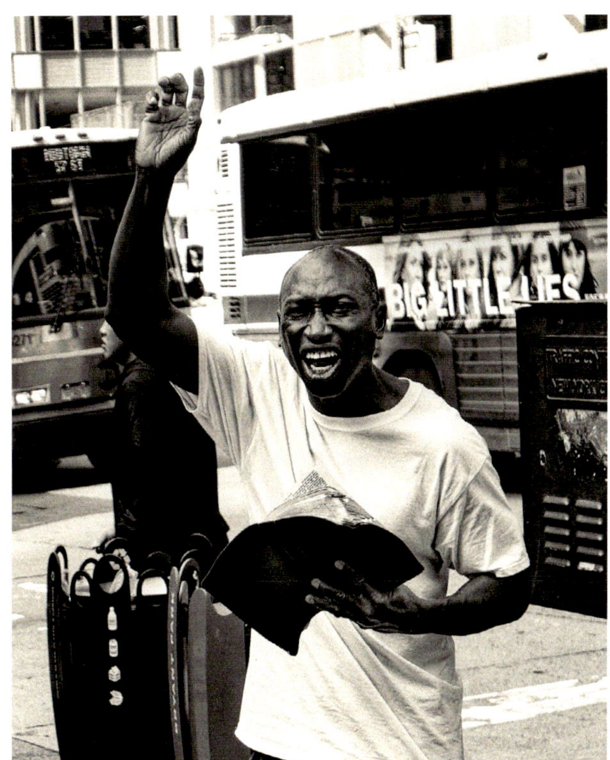

Once again, the dense clutter conspires to communicate provocative messages. Does the city embody an animistic consciousness that seeks to participate in the public dialogue? (6th Avenue at West 42nd Street.)

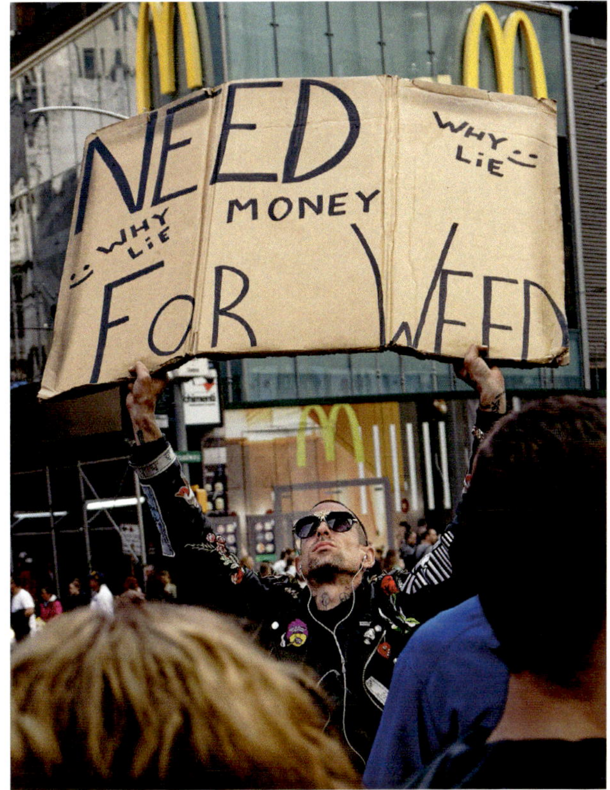

As preachers declare from the Bible the spiritual truth of an eternal hereafter, others announce from handwritten placards the fleshly truth of their worldly and temporal desires. The evangelists plead for your soul. The tokers beg for your money. (Times Square, Broadway at 45th Street.)

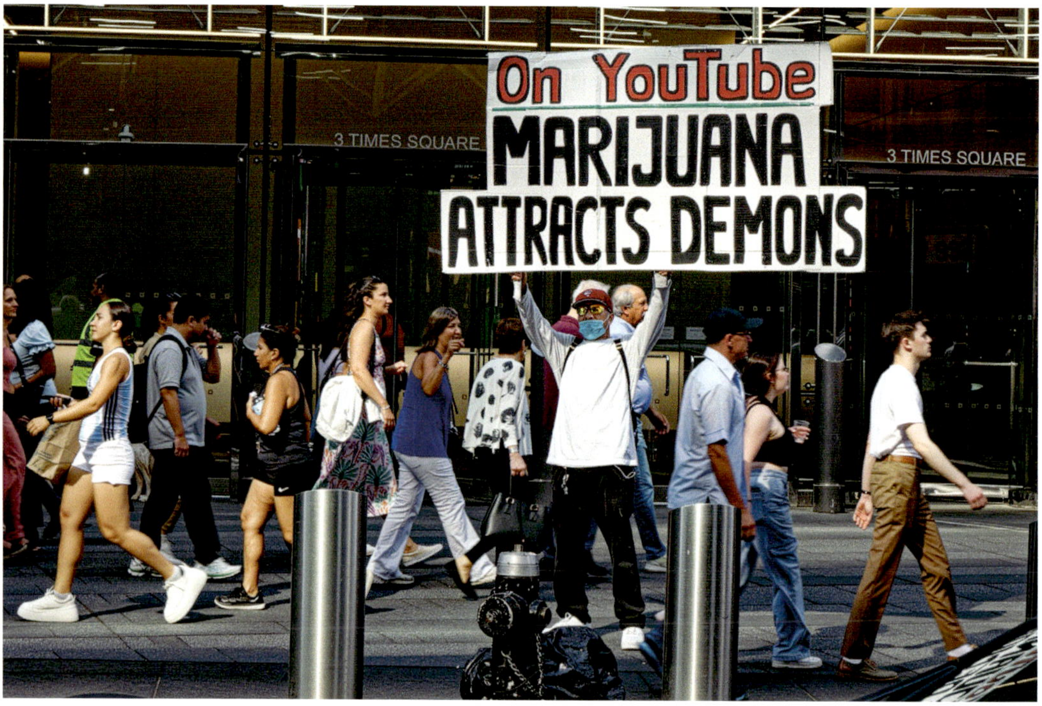

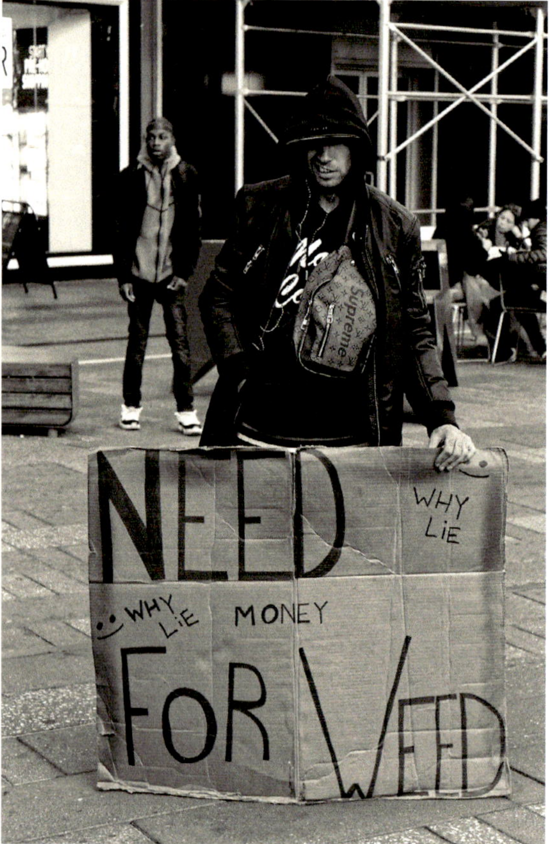

Above: The rhetoric escalates to hyperbolic intensity before a crowd that has grown numb to the daily proselytizing. (3 Times Square.)

Left: The clash is akin to a game of tennis between rival players, with each side hitting the truth back and forth as if it were a ball. (Times Square.)

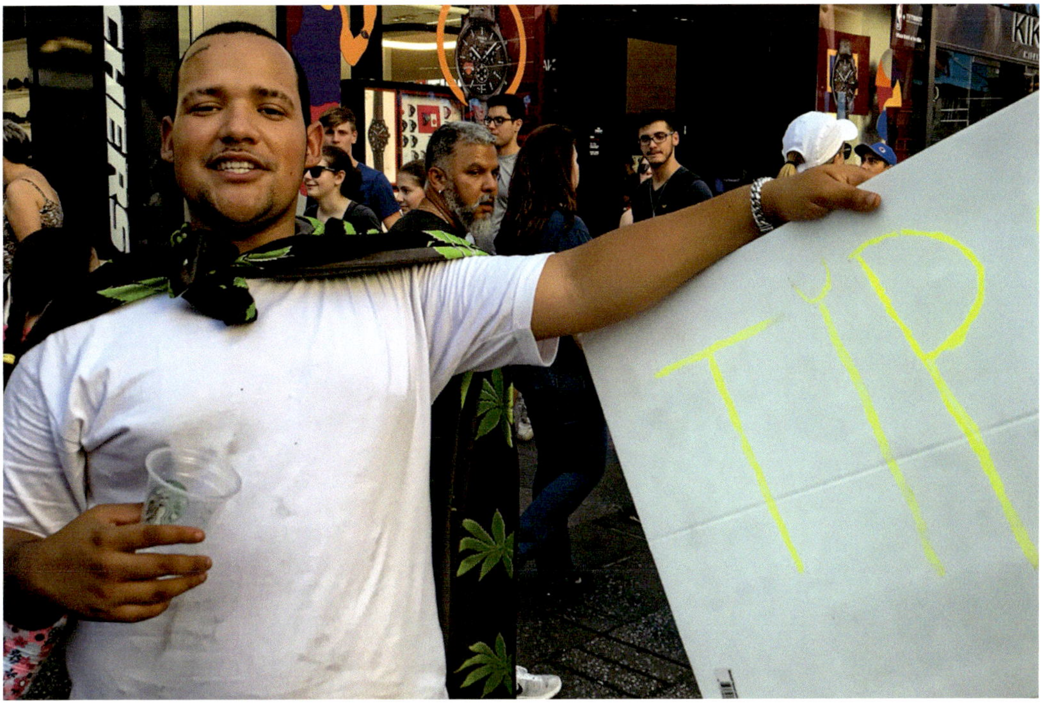

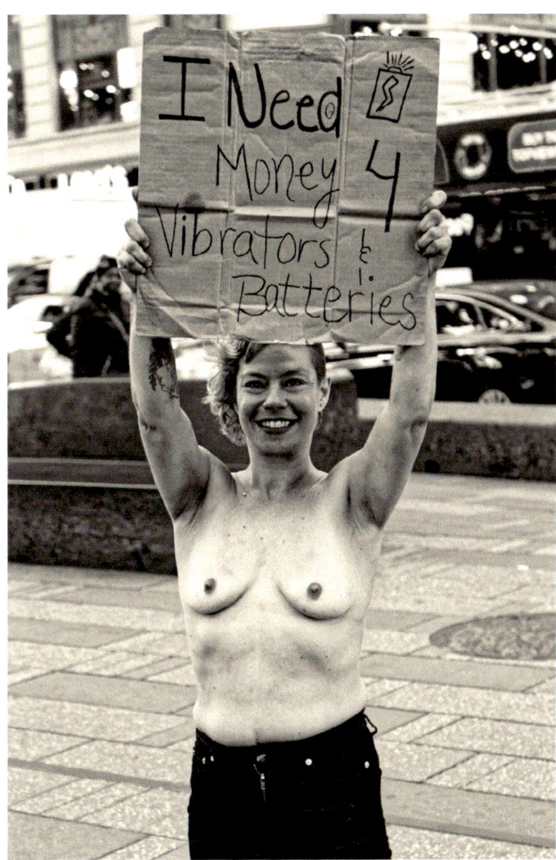

Above: For this cheerful fellow, though, he prefers to keep it simple with his one-word sign. That he is seeking advice is highly doubtful. (Times Square.)

Right: In the case of this happy New Yorker, the response she provokes is also thorny. Does she embody feminist empowerment by challenging certain taboos? Is she unwittingly reinforcing certain stereotypes? Could it be performance art or a comedic stunt? Maybe "a rose is a rose is a rose." (Times Square.)

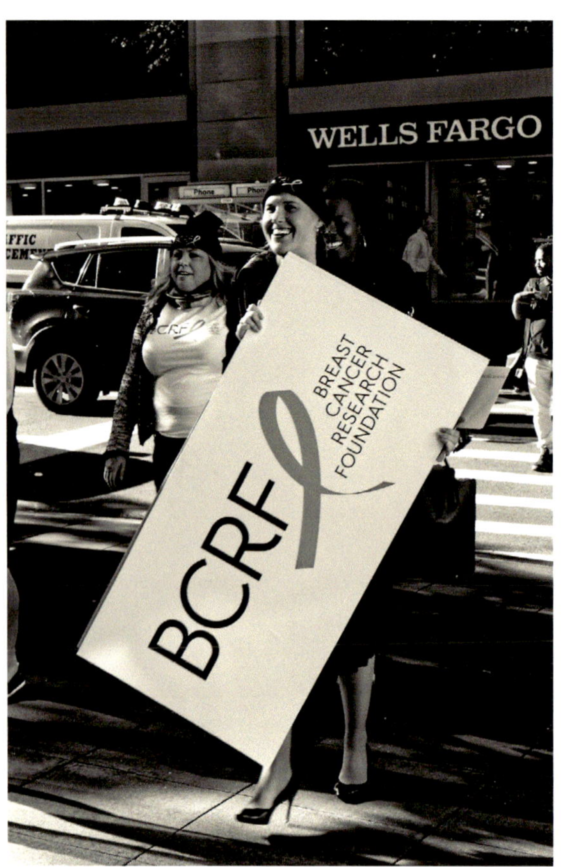

Left: Manhattanites have a lot to say and many ways to get their message across. A professionally designed and printed sign for a fundraiser makes for a great billboard during the walk to the event. (6th Avenue at West 45th Street.)

Below: A resourceful alternative is to print out a single-page flyer. It is in keeping with the grass roots tradition, going back to the Gutenberg press, of utilizing leaflets, pamphlets, and tracts to disseminate religious, political, and social ideas. (Times Square.)

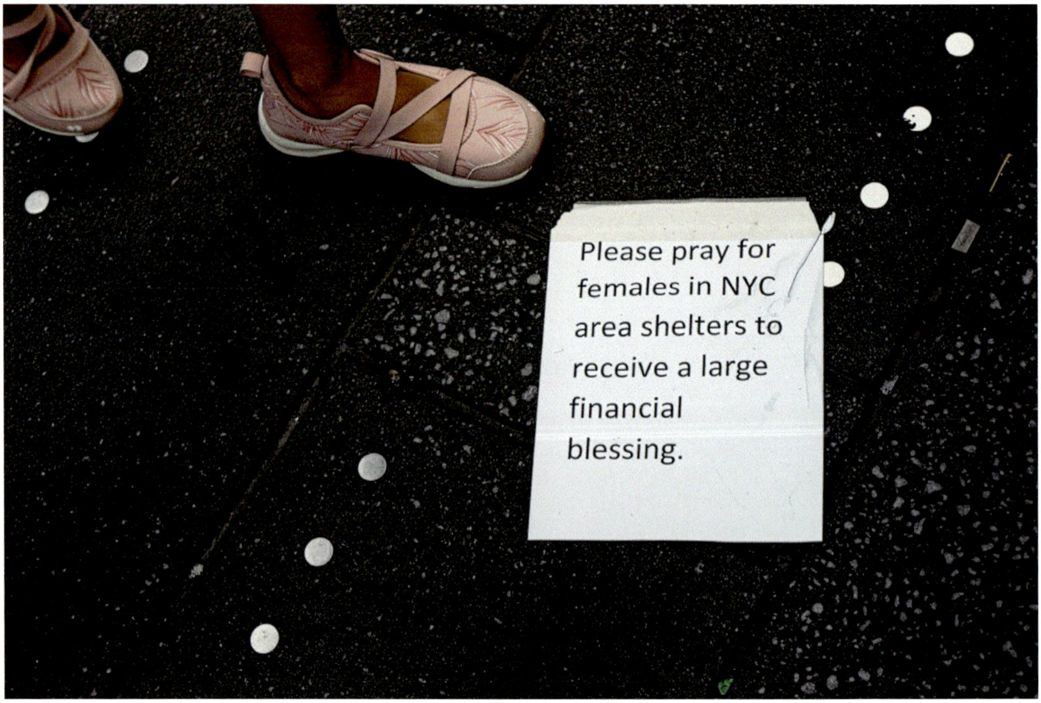

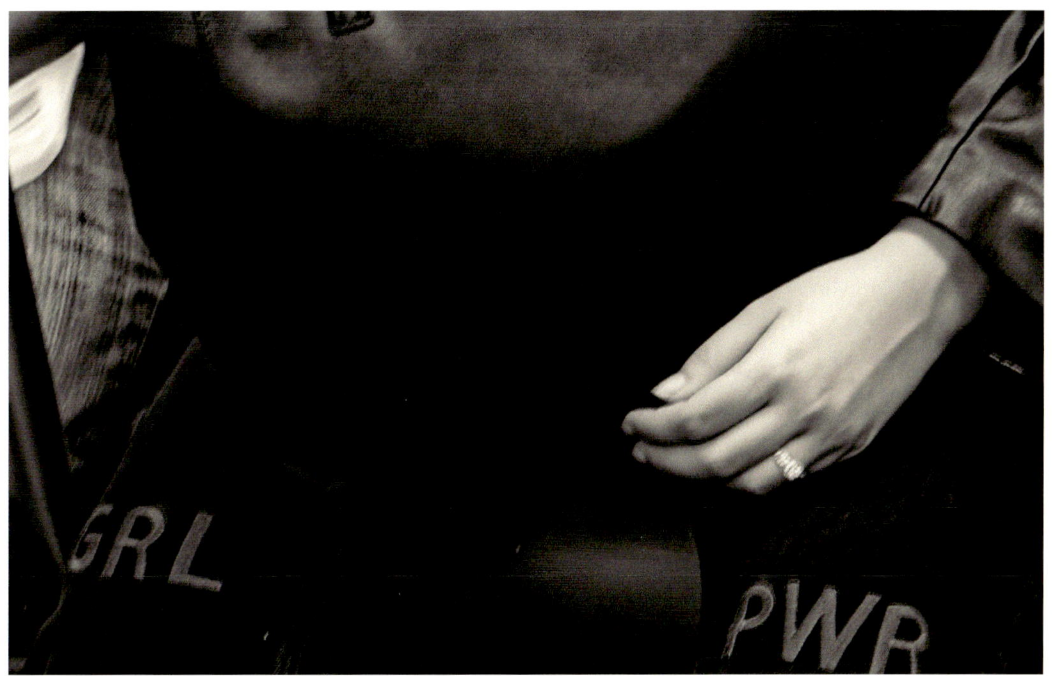

Clothing is yet another way. There are plenty of T-shirts displaying characters, catchphrases, and logos. Why not promote mindfulness of a political idea despite the manufacturer potentially exploiting the concept as a marketing strategy to target female consumers? (7 train, subway.)

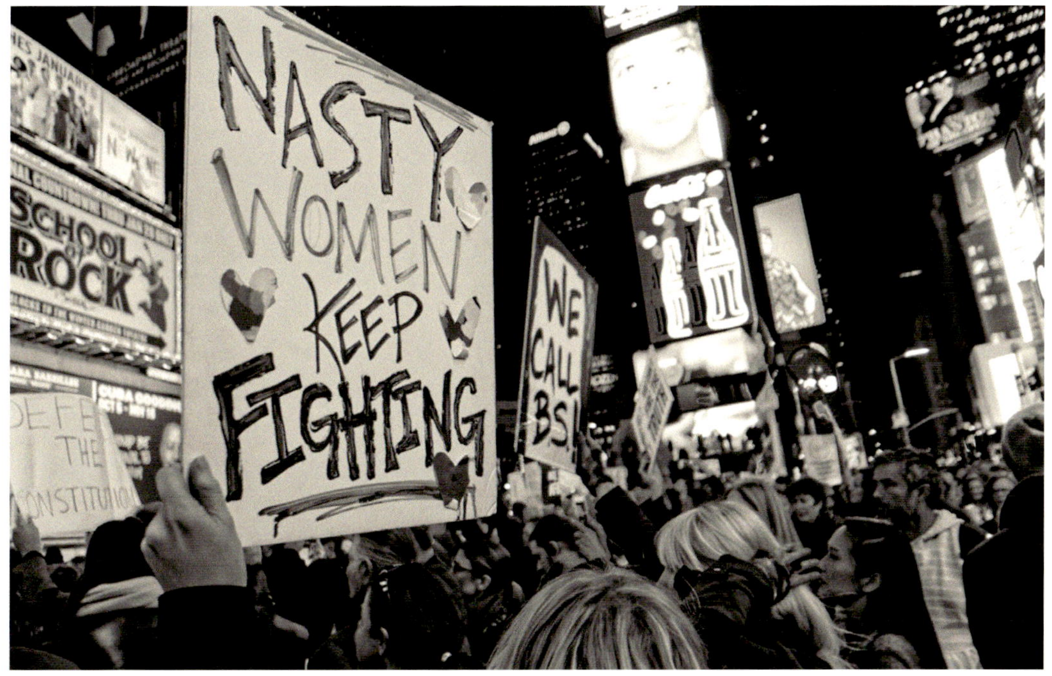

The emergence of social media has magnified the erosion of civility and the subversion of the republic. At the time of the 9/11 attacks, there were no online networks as we know them today. MySpace had not even launched yet. (Times Square.)

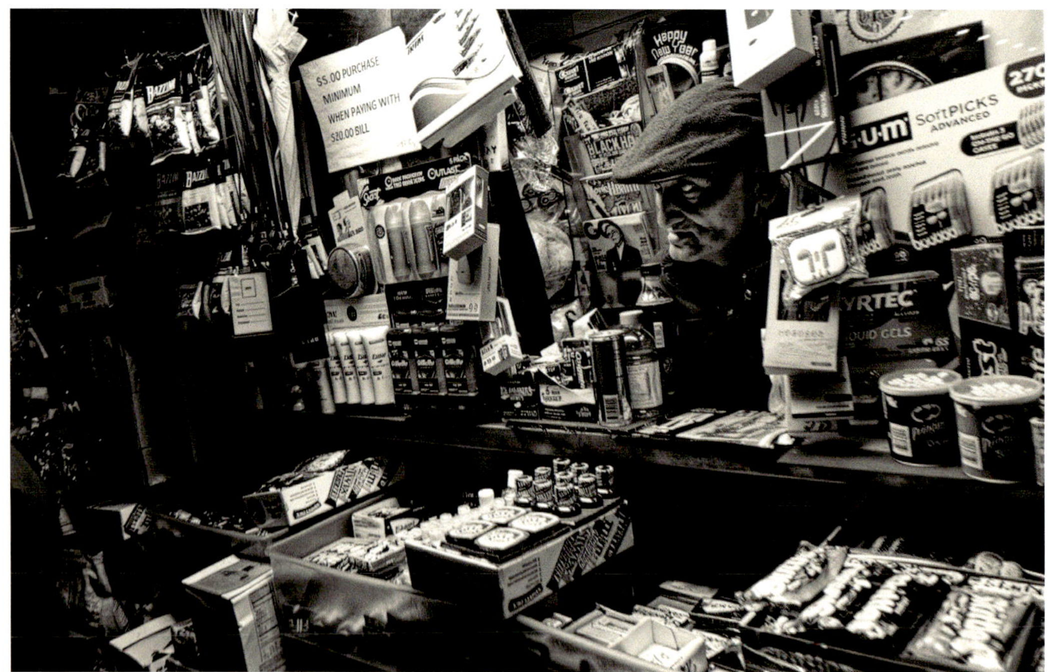

The concomitant decline of traditional news publications means that today's newsstands carry few papers and magazines. They are mostly selling soft drinks, snacks, candy, and other paraphernalia. These once-familiar sites are anachronisms that may eventually disappear altogether. Only a couple of hundred newsstands remain in Manhattan from over 1,000 in their 1950s heyday. (7th Avenue.)

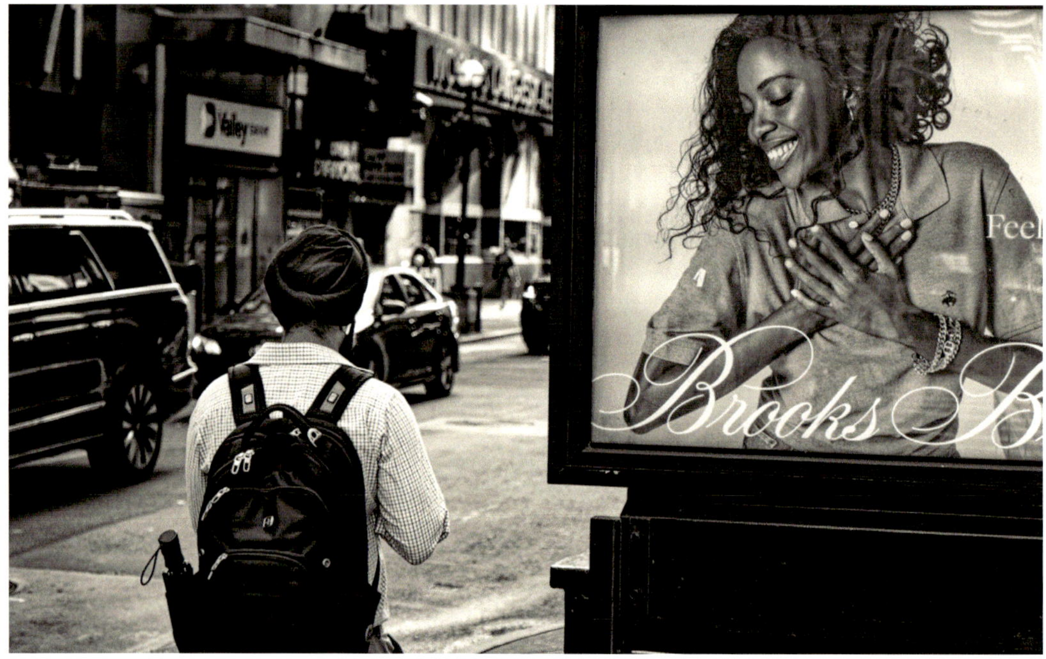

The rapid societal and cultural transformations have left Americans grappling for answers in the face of shifting ideas about identity, values, and norms. These big questions zoom down and impact common yearnings—the search for loving relationships, community and belonging, wellness and personal fulfillment. (6th Avenue at West 47th Street.)

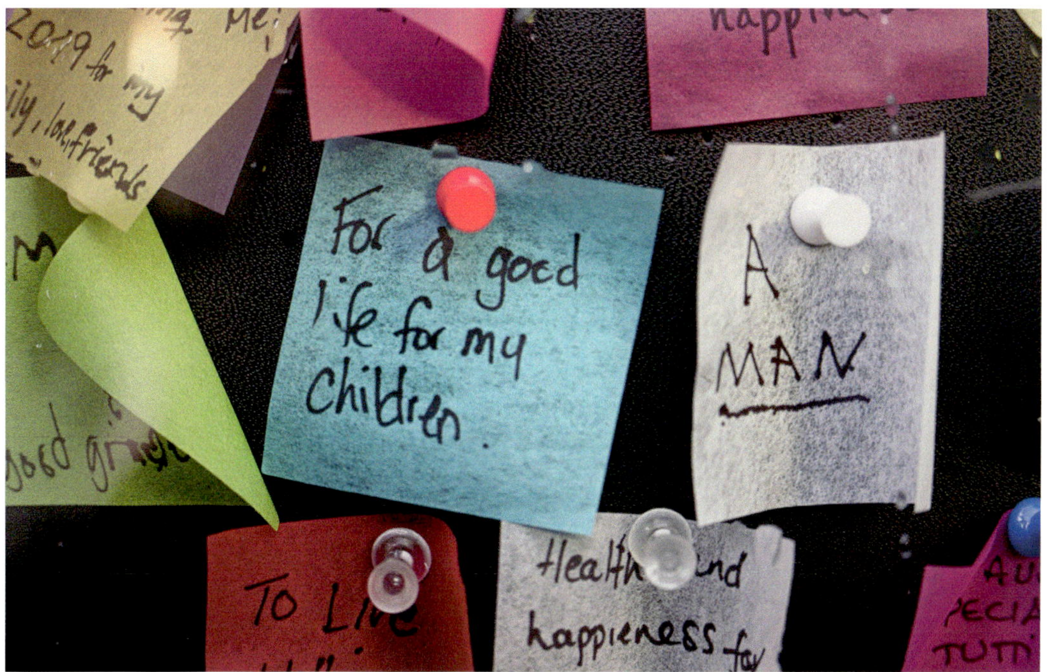

Above: We can see these wants scribbled on colored squares of paper pinned on the "Wishing Wall." They are all gathered to flutter down when the ball drops on New Year's Eve. (Times Square.)

Right: For some, their resolution is a daily commitment to humbly seek basic and immediate needs such as food, housing, and healthcare. (Times Square.)

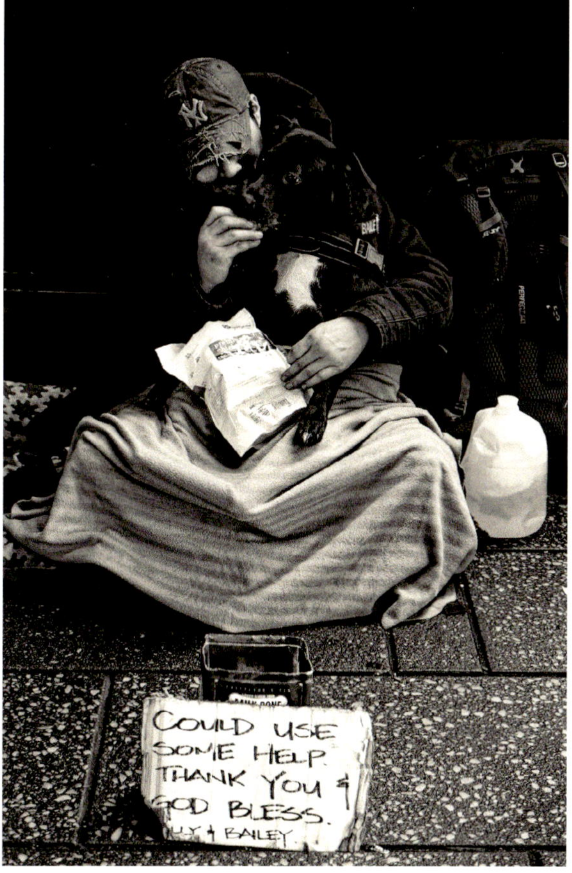

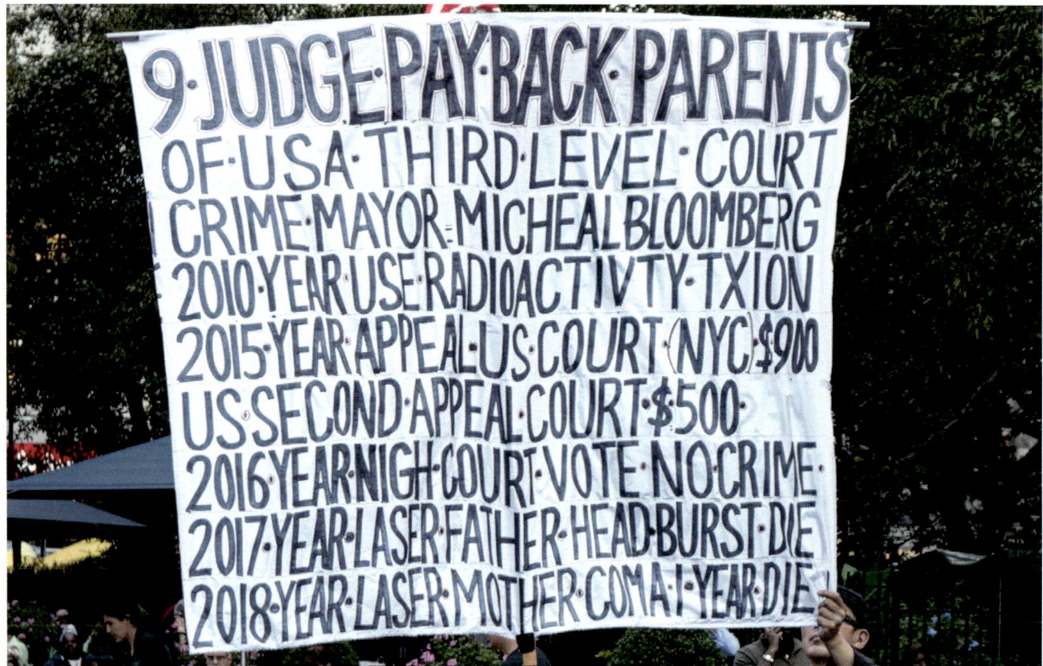

Others just want to be heard as they struggle to make sense of what they want to say. Social media is prevalent, yet many people still have a hidden desire to engage directly with others in the real world. (Herald Square, 6th Avenue at 34th Street.)

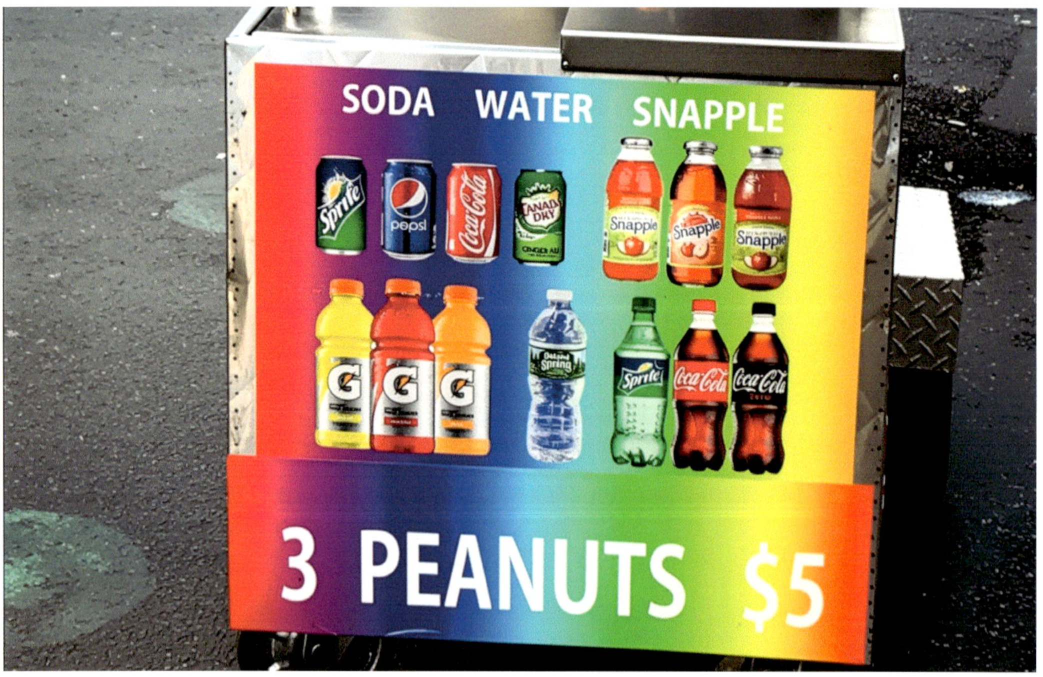

Perhaps we can more clearly see our way out of a foreboding mood by noticing the humor and levity around us. Are those three peanuts so large as to justify a whopping $5? (6th Avenue at West 33rd Street.)

Dancing and free pizza are sure to provide a welcome respite from the dilemma, fear, anxiety, and tension being faced. It just might be that it is during those moments of contentment that we come upon a way to keep the American dream alive. (Times Square.)

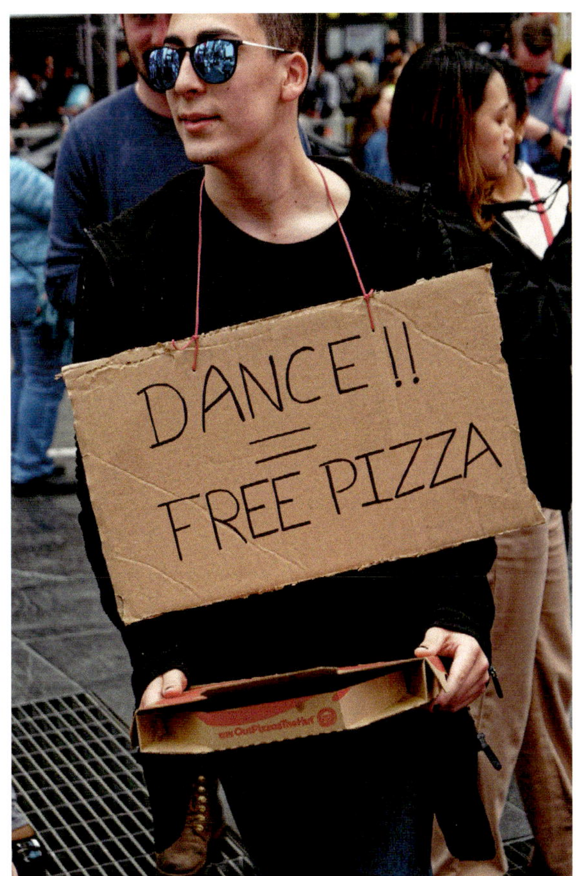

We may have significant differences, but we should all be able to agree with the Declaration of Independence that "We hold these truths to be self-evident, that all men are created equal, that they are endowed by their Creator with certain unalienable Rights, that among these are Life, Liberty and the pursuit of Happiness." (Broadway at West 37th Street.)

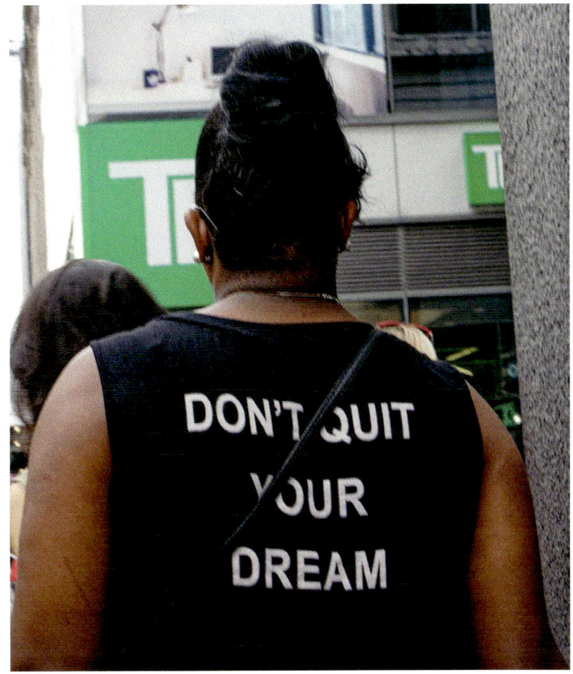

3

Small Things in a Big City

As I explained, I was so engrossed in my own little world that I did not even notice two G-stringed young women approaching me. The Big Apple has much to uncover. So do other places on earth.

"There are eight million stories," concludes *The Naked City*, a 1948 film set in Manhattan. The movie's tagline remains true today. I thought it was peculiar, then, when an acquaintance saw my photography and said, "You need to travel to be challenged by different cultures and lifestyles." He forwarded social media links of friends who visited developing nations in Asia. Their "fabulous" snapshots featured predictable scenes captured by countless other tourists. There were shots of food, statues, monkeys, and exotic landscapes. The pictures were not bad. They were pleasing and easy to look at precisely because the subject matter and compositions were familiar. But to me, whatever challenge they encountered by spending a few days in a foreign country was not reflected in their images.

The real issue is about rediscovering or reimagining the stories concealed within our present surroundings. It is understandable that as we fall into our daily routines, we become blind to subtleties and get bored. Seeking new experiences elsewhere becomes enticing. The thing is that for the folks living in that "elsewhere," a visit to your town or city may be an exciting escape from their humdrum world.

Landmarks and attractions often obscure smaller, interesting features. Such details can also be found in more modest locations. Scattered throughout New York are architectural ornamentations that are as much a form of public art as the rotating exhibits presented in Madison Square Park and along Broadway. Colors, shapes, and patterns are ever-changing elements appearing on structures and people. Seasons, weather, location, and time of day create more iterations. These factors go beyond the standard tourist attractions and reveal the city's true character.

It takes a deliberate effort to wander and hunt for these hidden urban stories. Virginia Woolf understood this. In "Street Haunting," she explains the necessity of inventing "an excuse for walking half across London." Woolf's pretext? "Really I must buy a pencil." She humorously acknowledges the guilt felt in pursuing such a leisurely activity. It is why "the golfer plays in order that open spaces may be preserved from the builders." That is the kind of challenge that can deepen our appreciation for our surroundings, enrich our travels, and give our photographs a more authentic representation of our experiences.

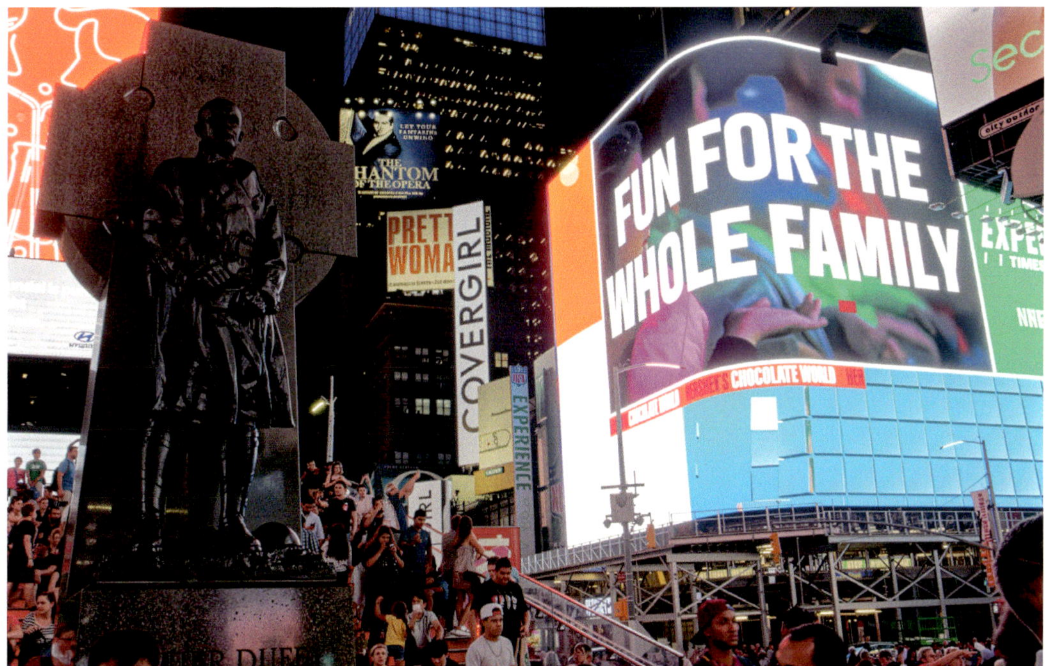

The city has so much to offer that it can be easy to superficially focus attention on the iconic places featured in movies and social media. (Times Square.)

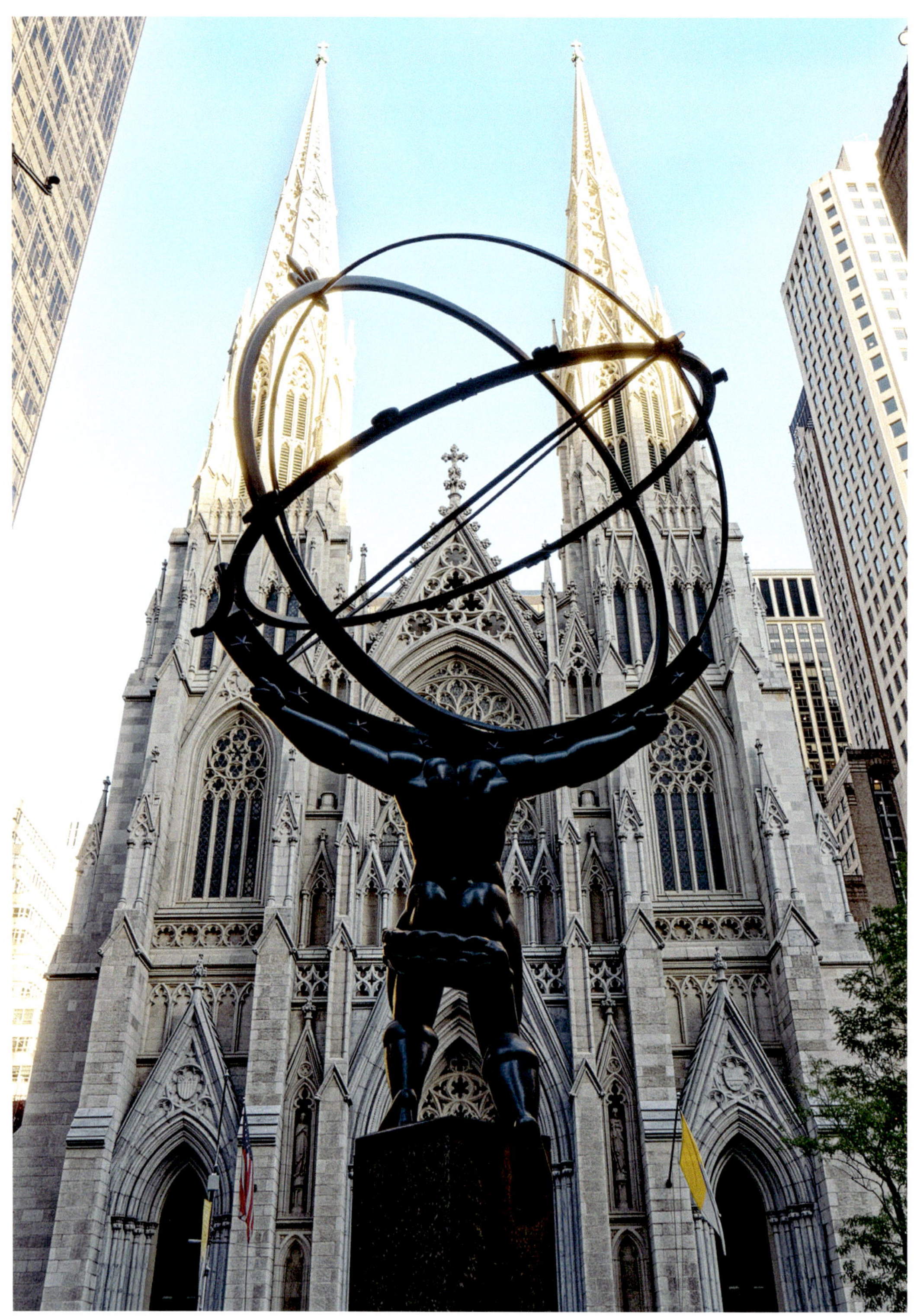

A studious look at a famous site, like the statue of Atlas, takes on a new perspective and meaning when viewed from behind and against the backdrop of another celebrated landmark like St. Patrick's Cathedral. (Rockefeller Center.)

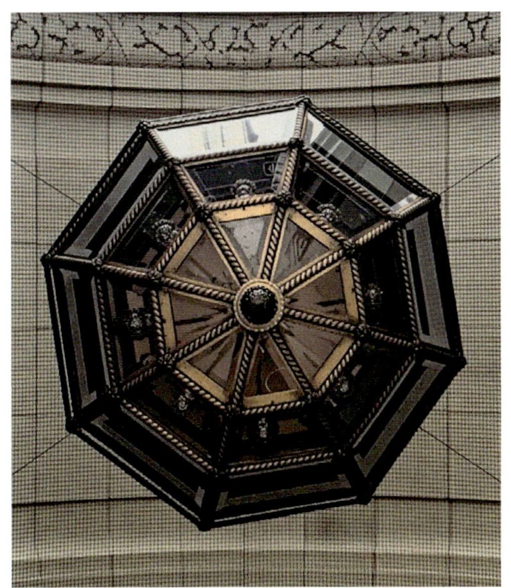 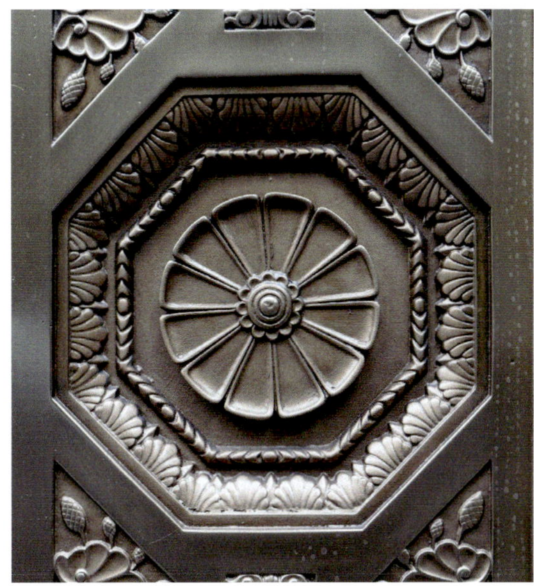

Above left: Sometimes the appreciation of a seemingly mundane element, such as this chandelier, heightens the beauty of the whole. (New York Public Library, 5th Avenue.)

Above right: It is illuminating to get close and become aware of subtle architectural details, a floret for example, and consider how its shape echoes those seen elsewhere. (Fred F. French Building, 5th Avenue.)

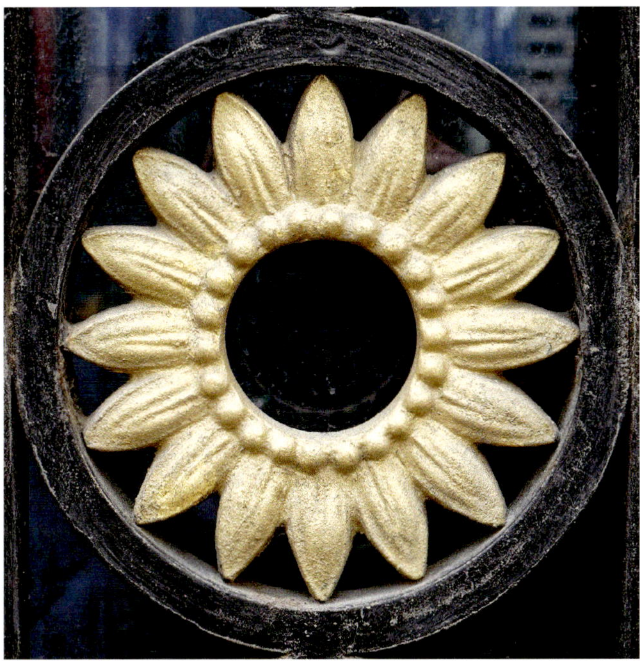

Rosettes, on the other hand, are a more elaborate ornamentation as seen here on the metalwork of a gate-like doorway. (Harry Winston jewelry store, 5th Avenue.)

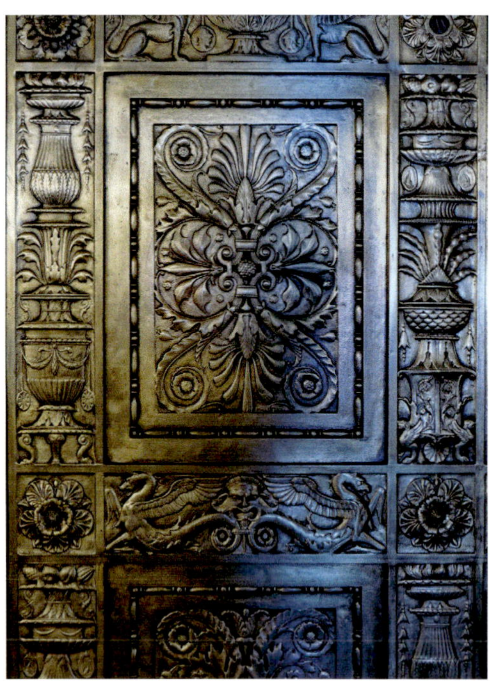

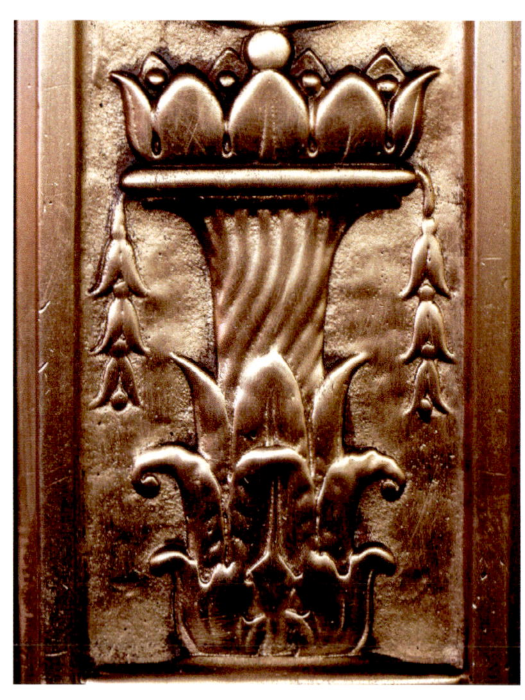

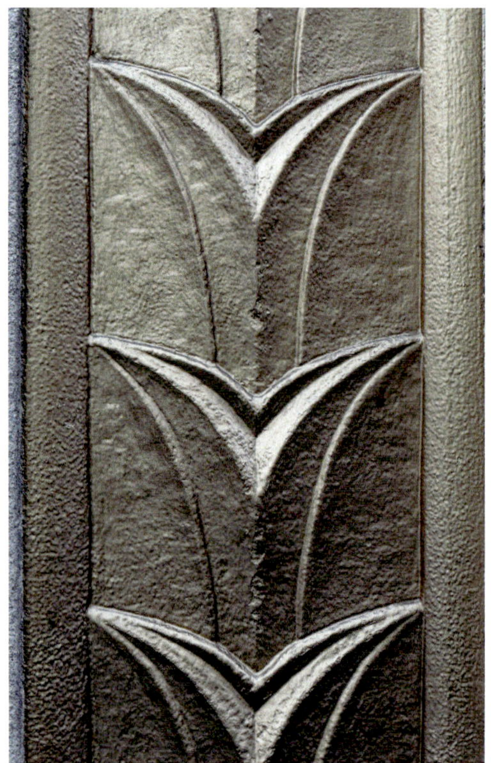

Above left: Many pass by or enter through the doors of this event space without noticing the elegant and intricate filigree designs that have been cast, engraved, and polished onto a canvas of brass. (Gotham Hall, Broadway.)

Above right: Other engraved motifs incorporate artfully ornate figures inspired by nature and classical Greek or Roman influences. (Paramount Building, Times Square.)

Left: A stylized rendering of wheat creates a pattern that is, at once, organic as well as geometric and abstract. (Fred F. French Building, 5th Avenue.)

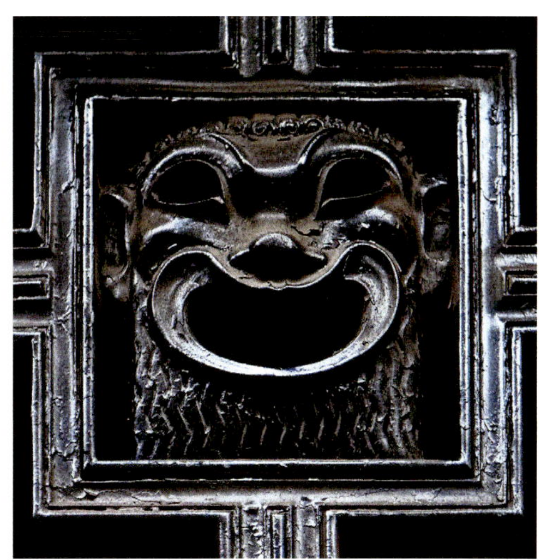

The Radio City Music Hall façade is so familiar that it takes a sharp eye to notice the faces within the grating above the stage entrances. (51st Street at 6th Avenue.)

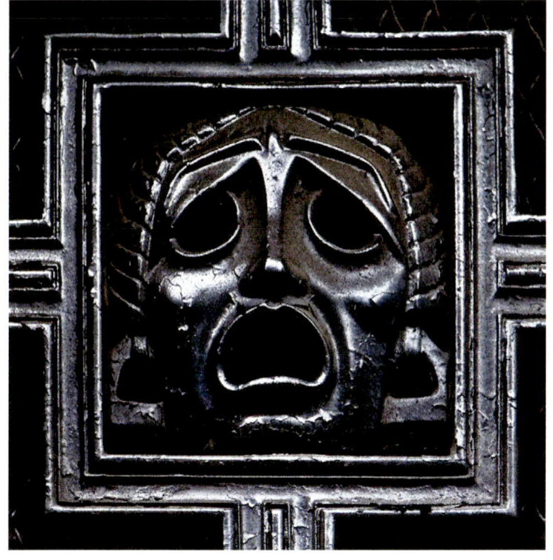

In ancient Greece, actors wore masks with exaggerated features so that audiences could tell from a distance what emotions were involved in the scene. (51st Street at 6th Avenue.)

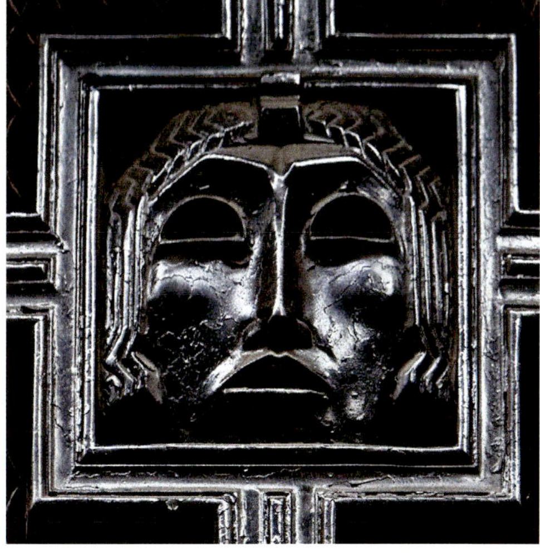

The comedy and tragedy masks now symbolize the theater. Mysteriously, a third mask also appears. Perhaps it is a design of the music hall's own making representing wonder or a mood between the extremes of laughter and grief. (51st Street at 6th Avenue.)

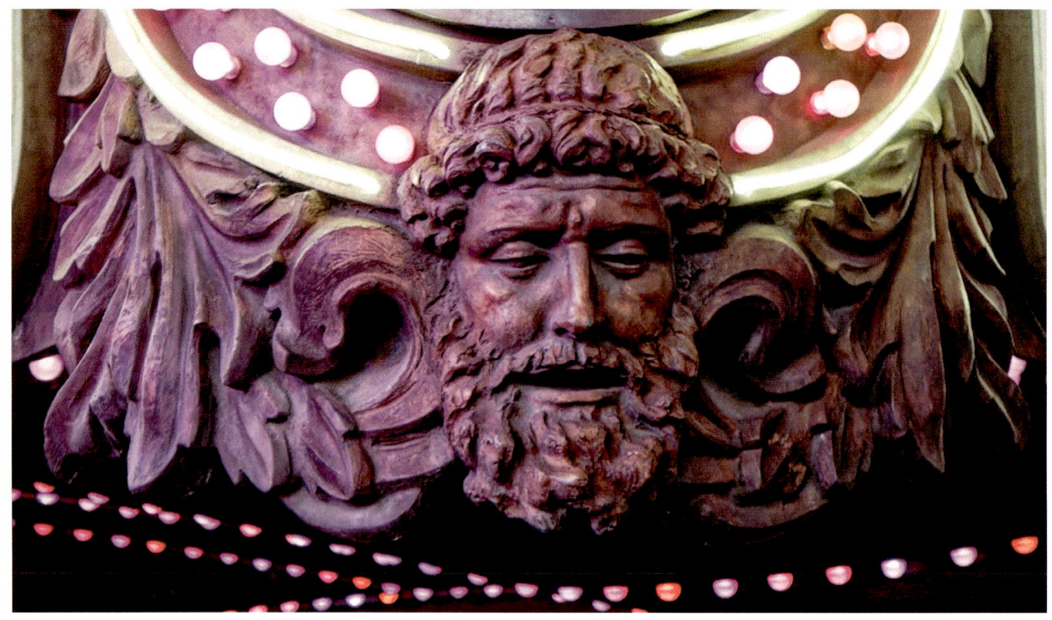

Above: A more realistic representation of a theatrical mask, with an obvious nod to Greece, can be observed tucked into the corners of this marquee. (Paramount Building, Times Square.)

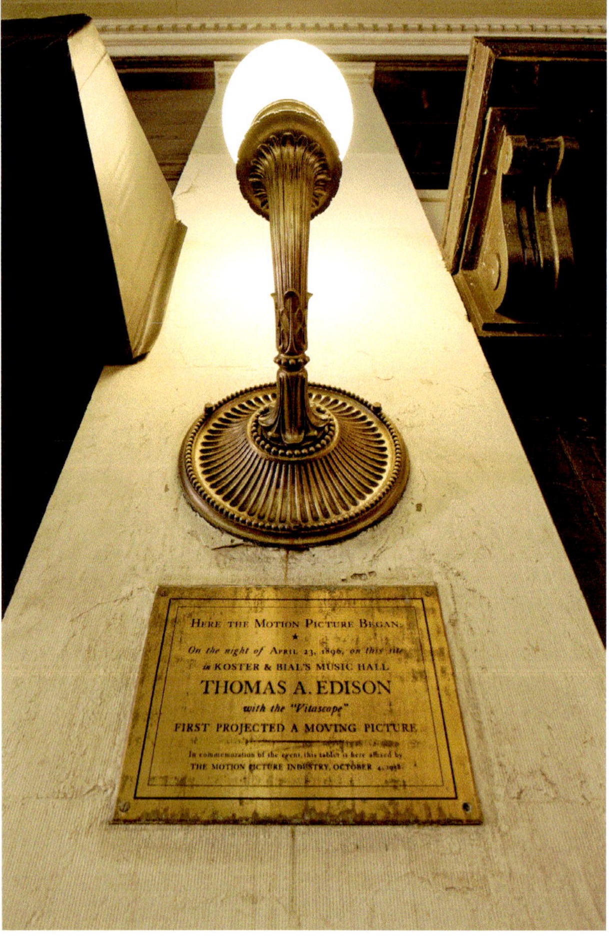

Left: Many points of interest, even within world-renowned landmarks, hover like unseen spirits above the heads of most New Yorkers and tourists. (Macy's, 34th Street between Broadway and 7th Avenue.)

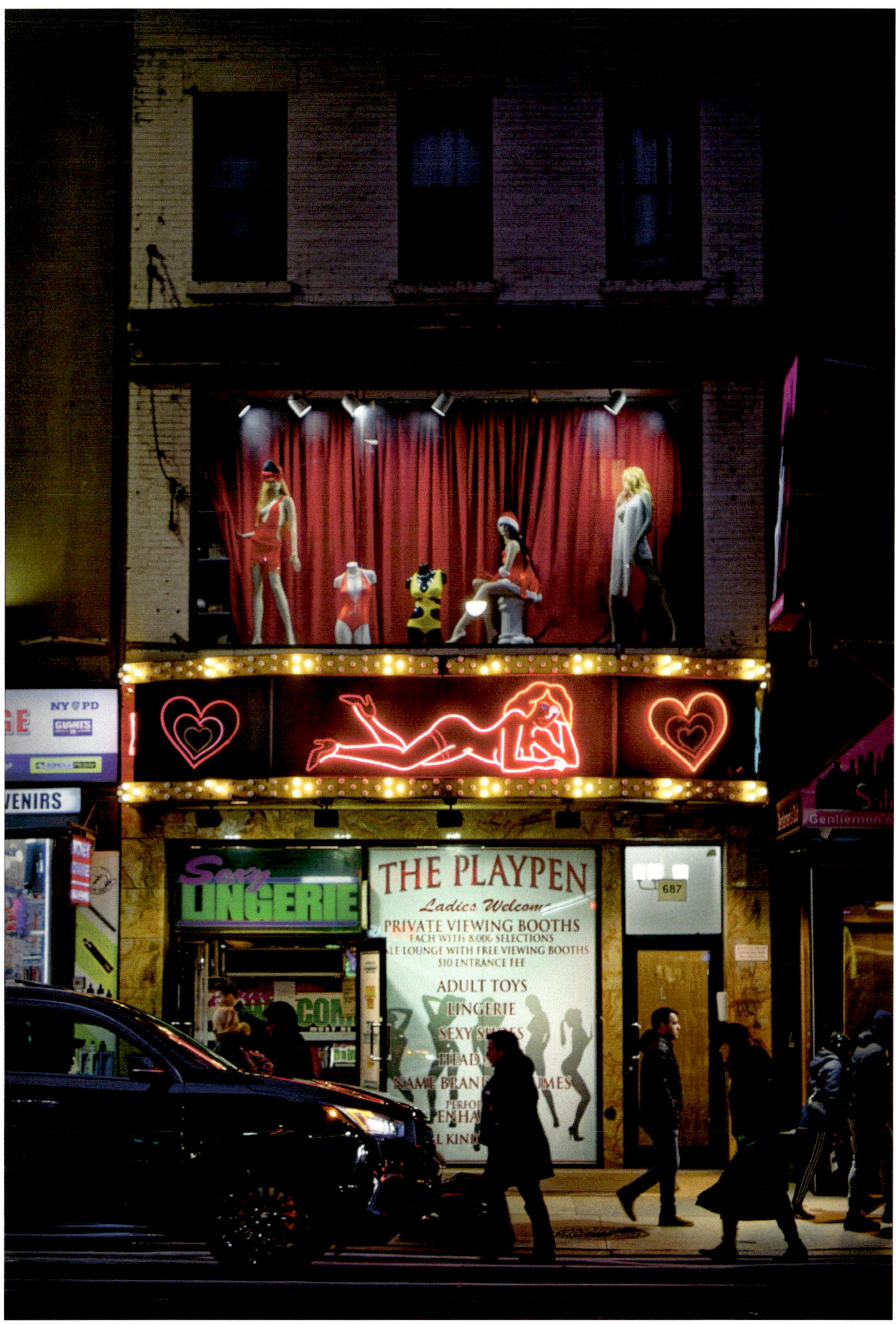

Periodically, ghosts are sighted from the city's past when Times Square was home to live performances and motion pictures of a seedier type. (The Playpen, 687 8th Avenue.)

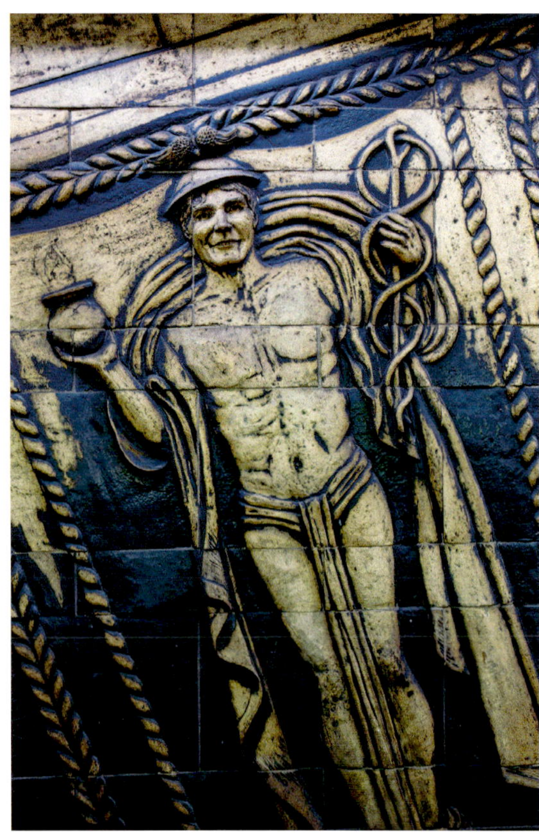

The face of this semi-nude relief of Hermes, who guides souls to the underworld, bears a curious resemblance to Harrison Ford. Or is it Steve Martin? Maybe the Tin Man from the Wizard of Oz? It is a detail easily overlooked by commuters rushing down the stairs to catch a train on the Long Island Railroad. (Tracks 20-21, Penn Station.)

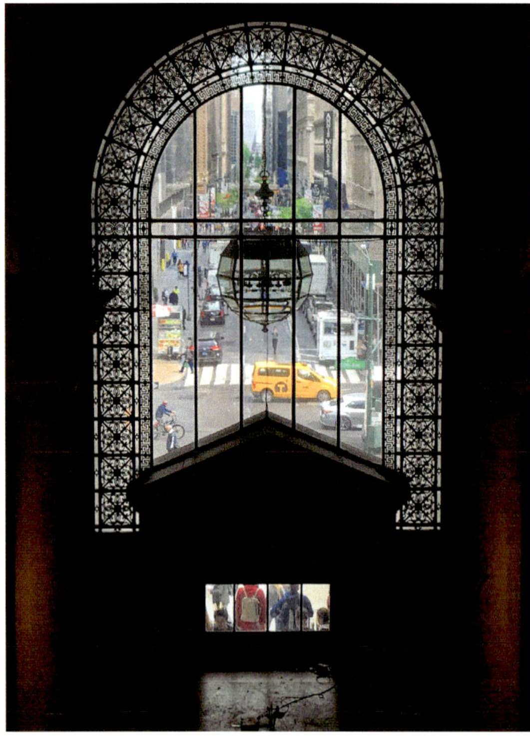

Pausing to take in the view through an arched window evokes the open feeling of being carried away through a portal. This shape, popular in Greek and Roman architecture, can be found throughout the city. (New York Public Library, 5th Avenue.)

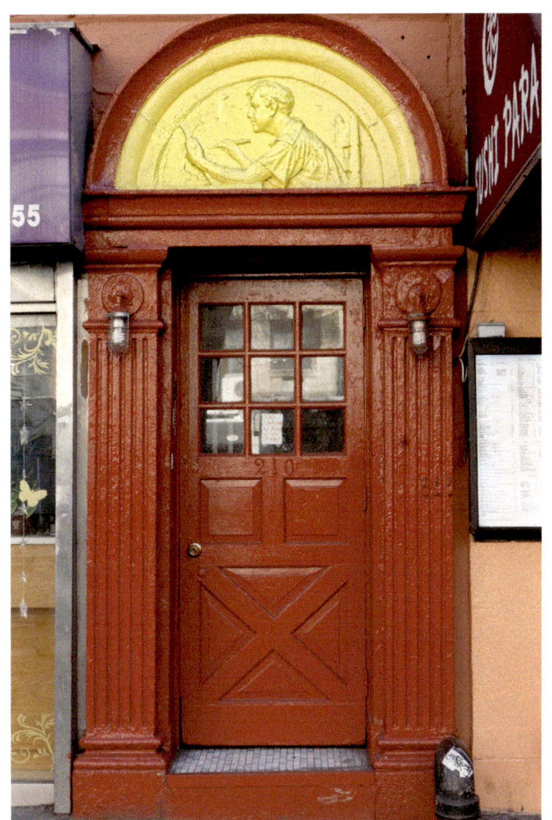

Other arches off the beaten path beckon us to enter history. The yellow tympanum on this Greek Revival row house memorializes its artist-owner, Pompeo Luigi Coppini, who rented studio space to French Dadaist Marcel Duchamp. (210 West 14th Street, Greenwich Village.)

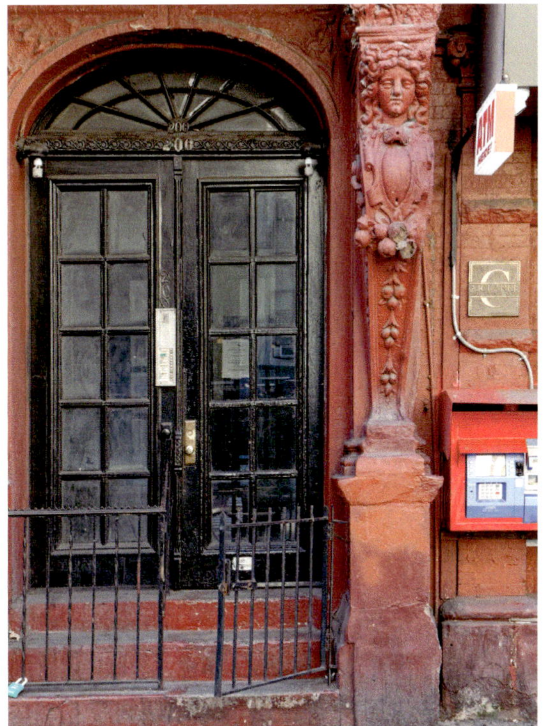

The face gracing another bright red exterior appears to be a caryatid, similar to the decorative pillars found on the Acropolis of Athens. (The Jeanne d'Arc Building, 200 West 14th Street, Greenwich Village.)

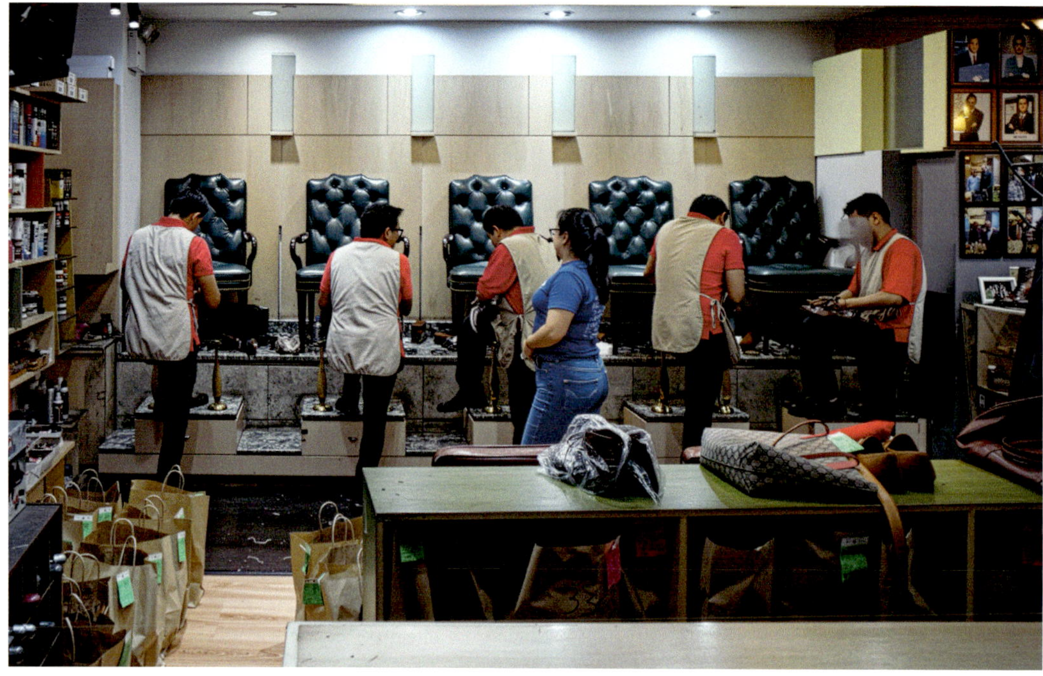

Flashes of red against blue in a busy shoeshine stand create fleeting moments of symmetry, motion, and serendipity. (Rockefeller Center Concourse.)

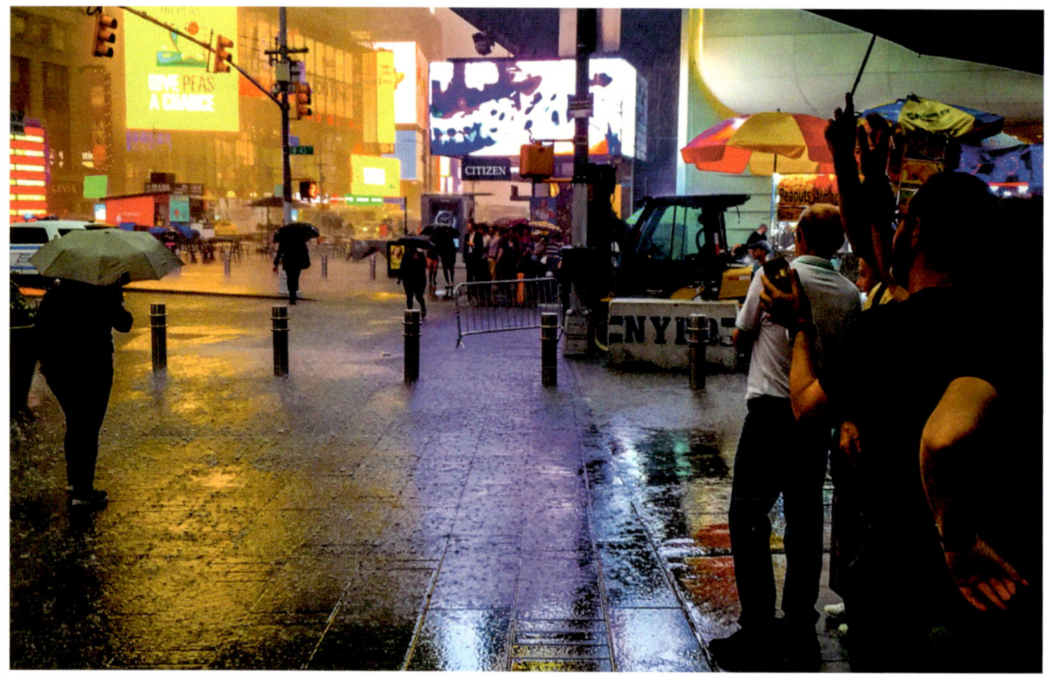

Instead of seeking shelter, braving a walk through a downpour offers a chance to see how nature's atmospherics transform a sense of place. (Times Square.)

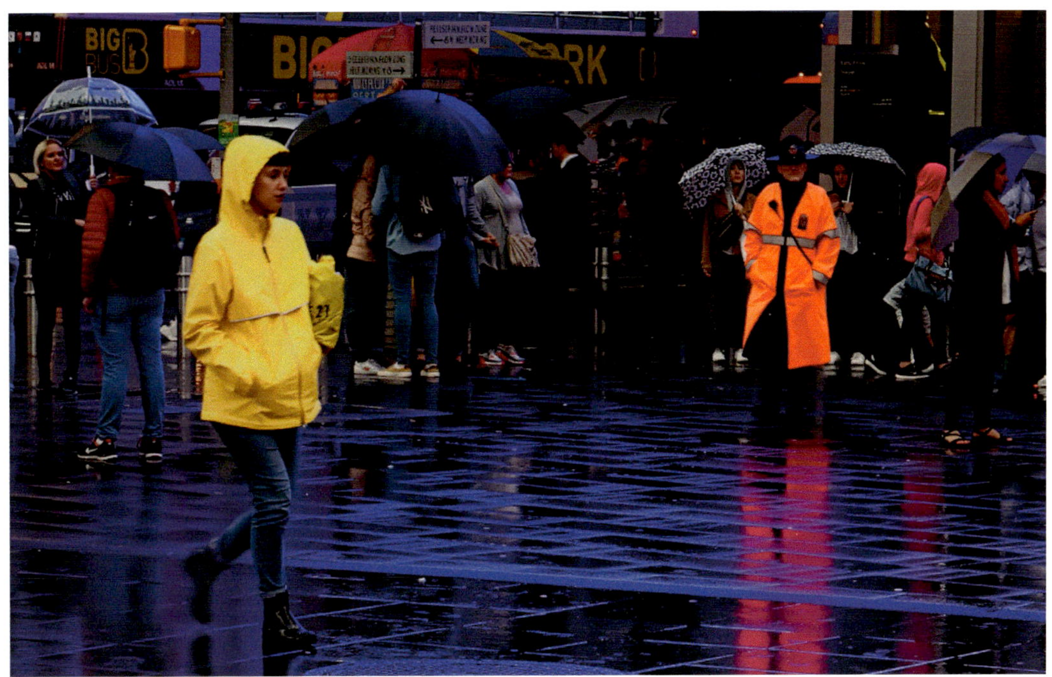

Colors become saturated and a neon world emerges as rain slickers and huge illuminated signs, known as "spectaculars," reflect off glistening streets. (Times Square.)

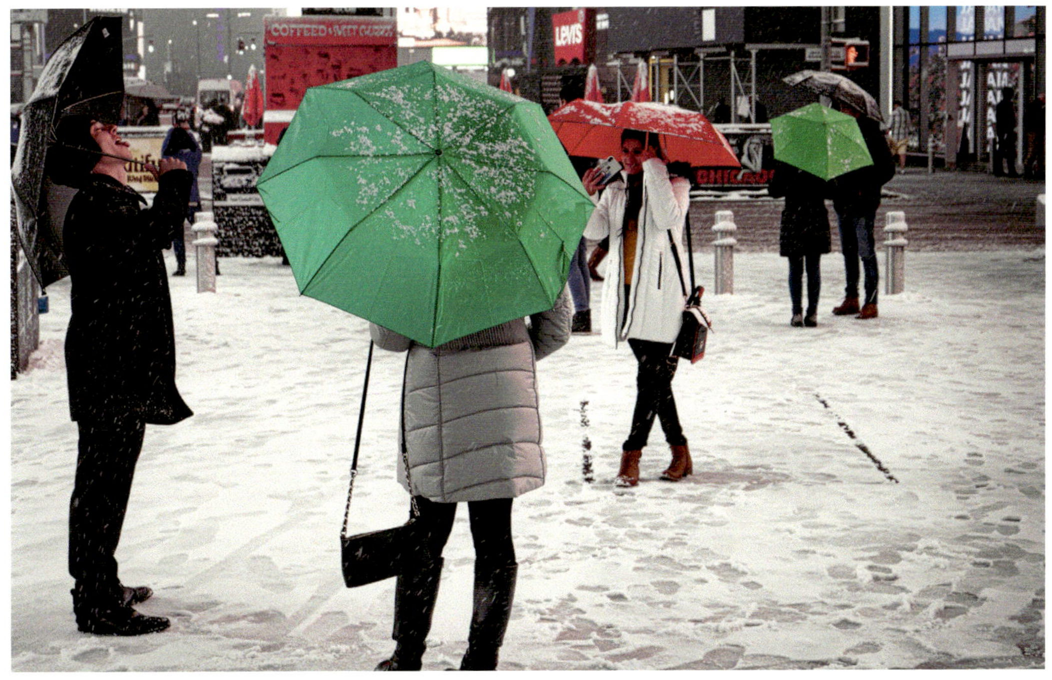

A blanket of snow creates a backdrop that makes patterns of complementary colors stand out to the keen observer. (Times Square.)

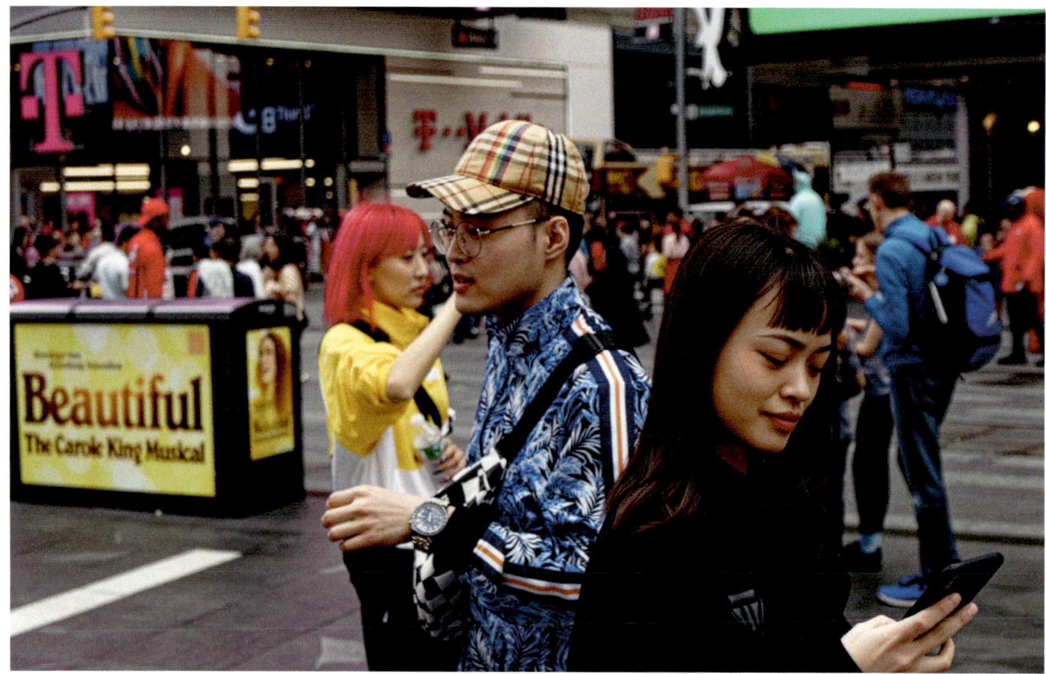

Primary colors occasionally collide on the street, creating a fleeting, vibrant arrangement that offers a delightful visual experience. (Times Square.)

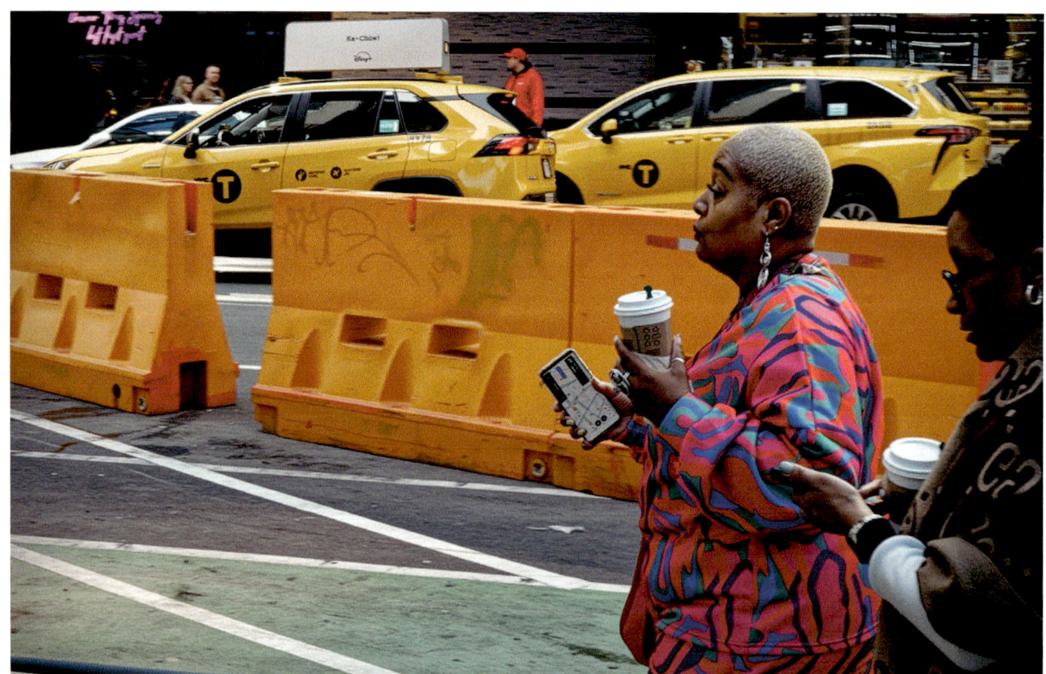

Artistic street scenes with bold contrasts and strong diagonals briefly come into view and vanish, inviting appreciation from those who are attentive. (7th Avenue at West 47th Street.)

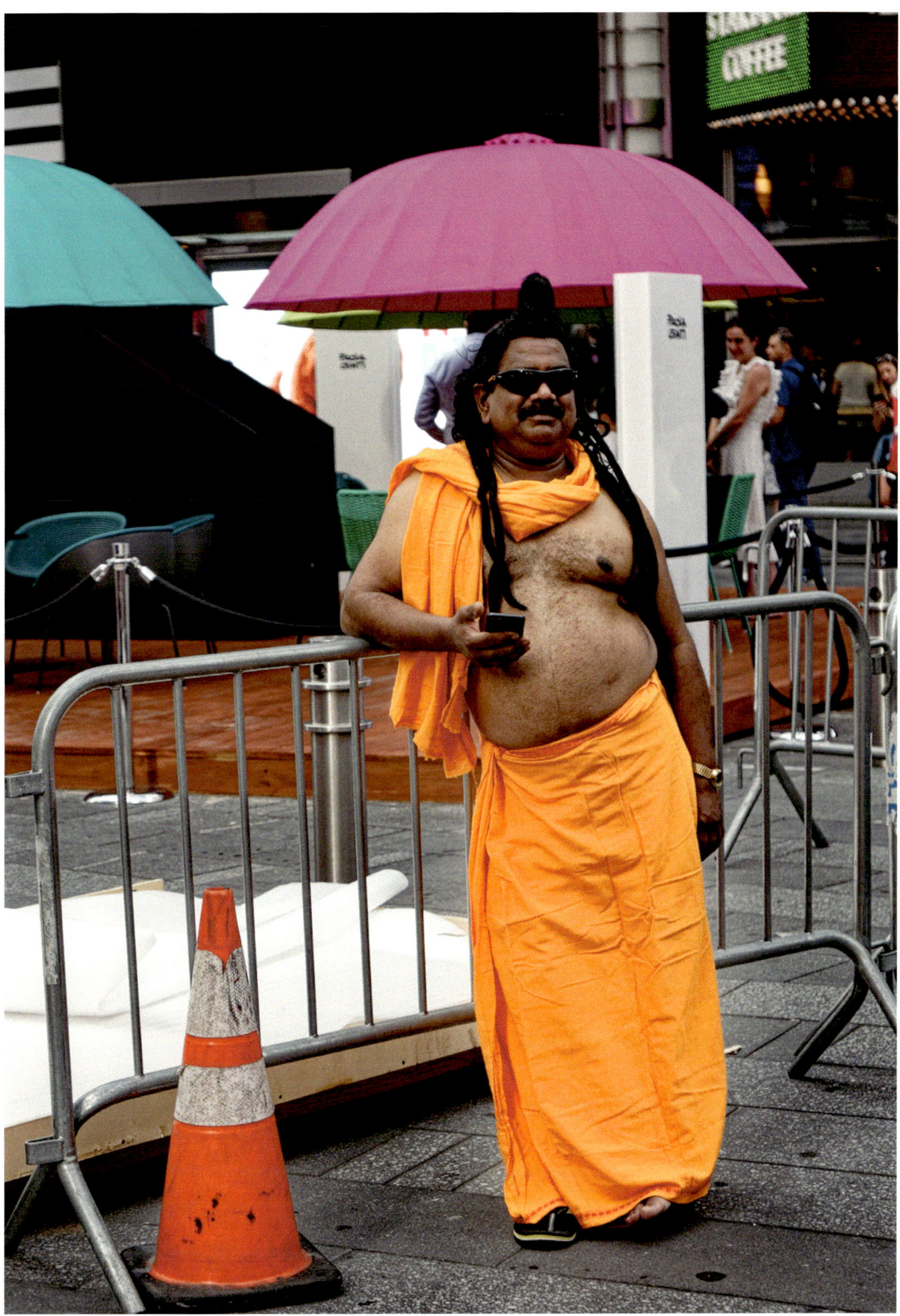

Turning a street corner can bring a sense of discovery, much like every twist of a kaleidoscope reveals a new, engaging composition. (Times Square.)

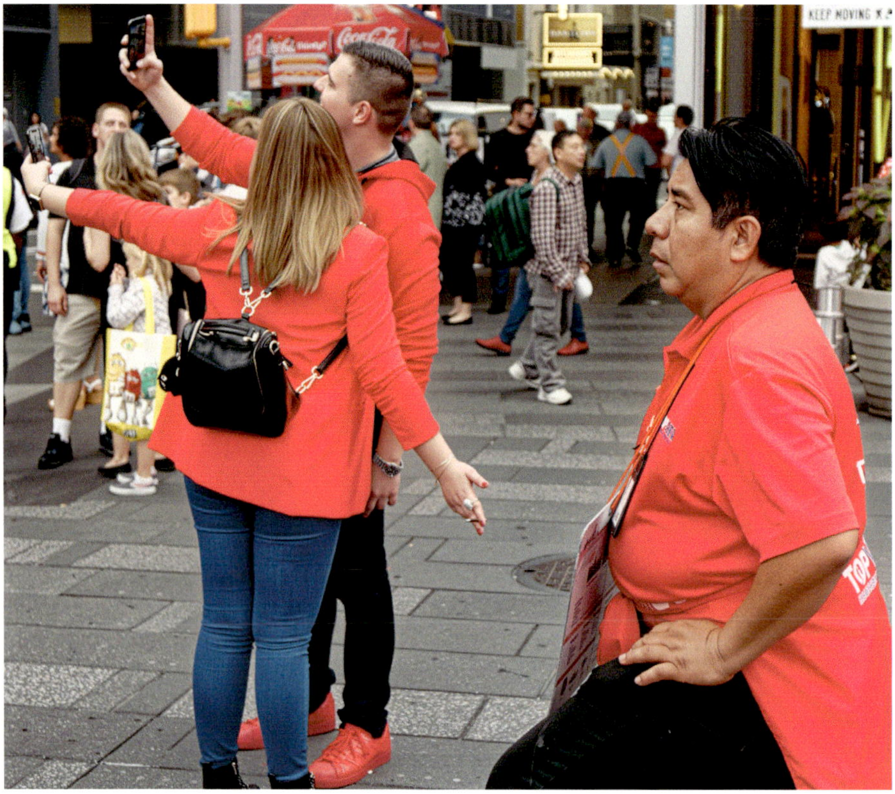

It is astonishing how colors can become randomly choreographed into layers that establish a pathway extending from the front of the scene to the back. (Times Square.)

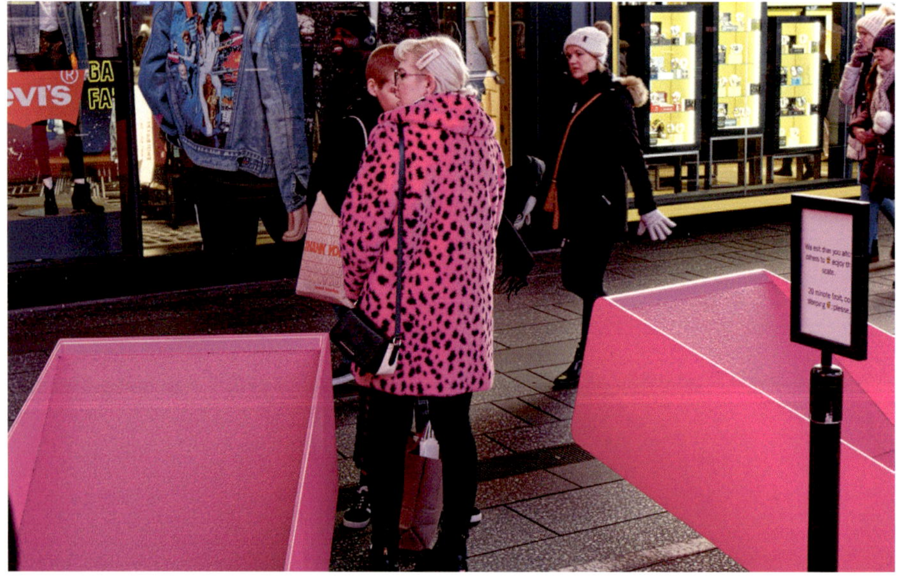

In music, the sound of one pitch might audibly trigger that same frequency or a harmonic of it in another nearby instrument. (Times Square.)

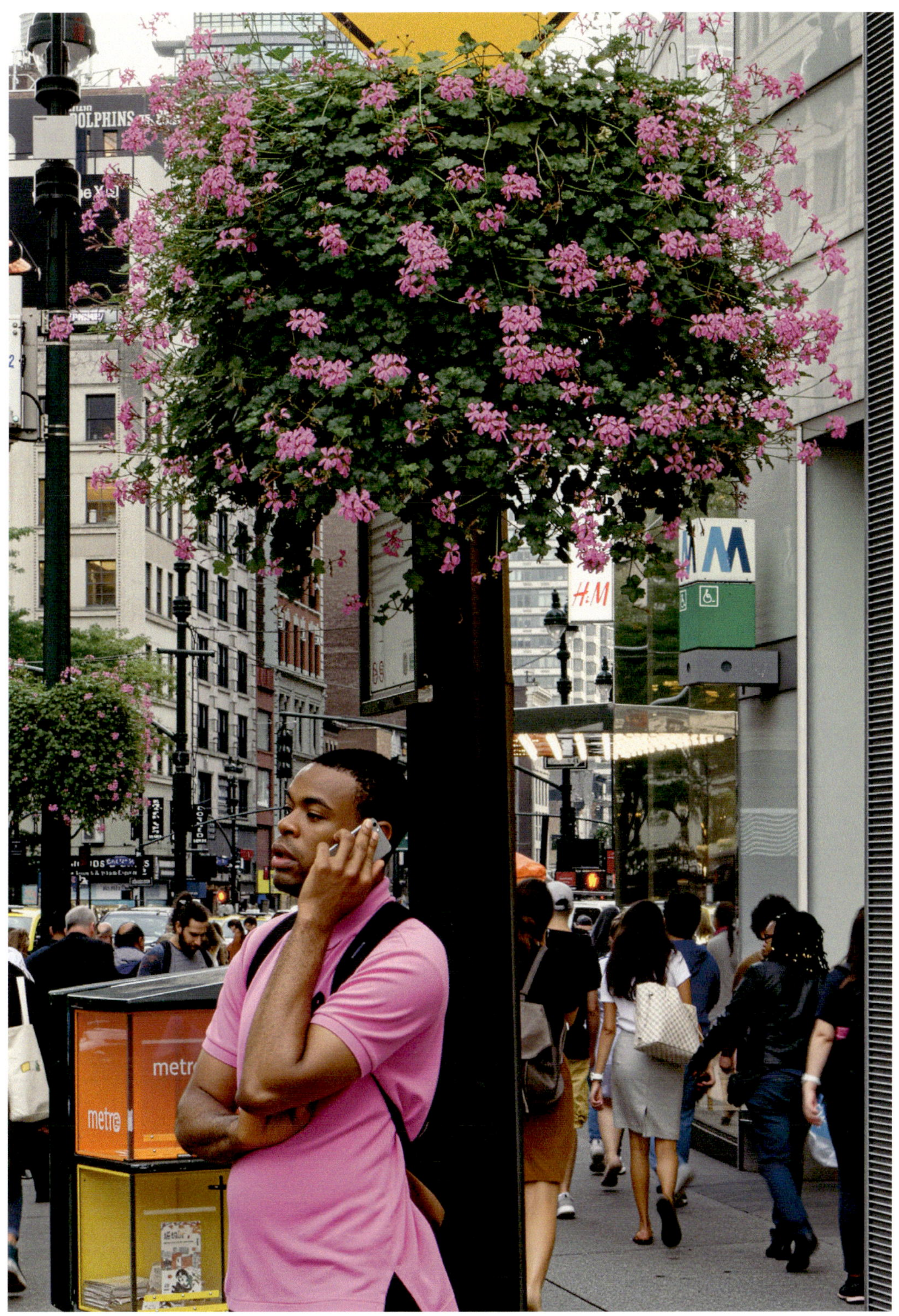

Similarly, the urbanscape seems to have an energy that tunes in and responds sympathetically to accentuate the richness of its surroundings. (Broadway at 34th Street.)

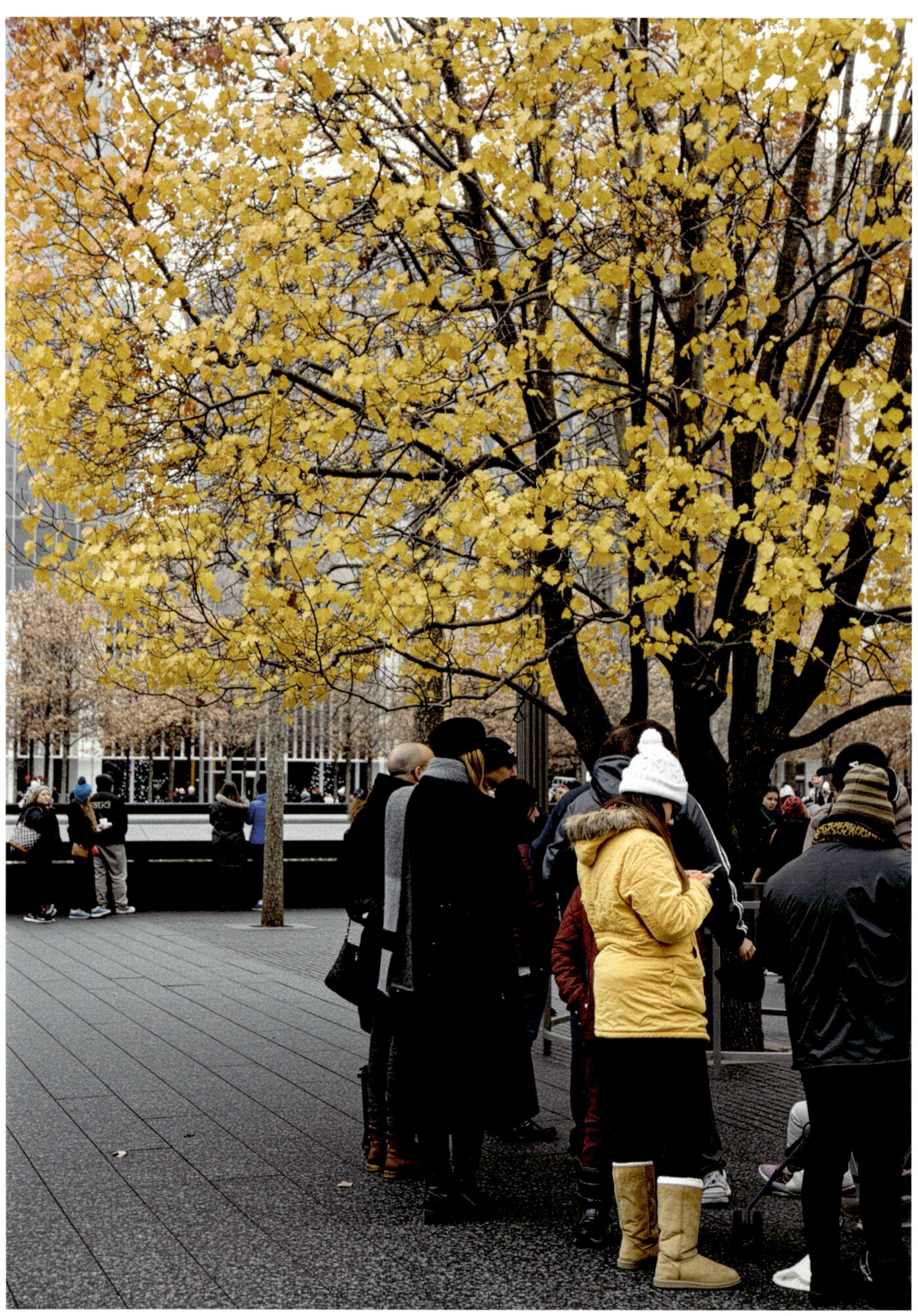

Is the Survivor Tree a manifestation of the spirits of those who perished on 9/11? Though charred and stumpy, the Callery pear tree discovered amidst the wreckage showed signs of life. Replanted in 2010, it blossoms each spring, embodying a living symbol of resilience. (South Pool, 9/11 Memorial and Museum.)

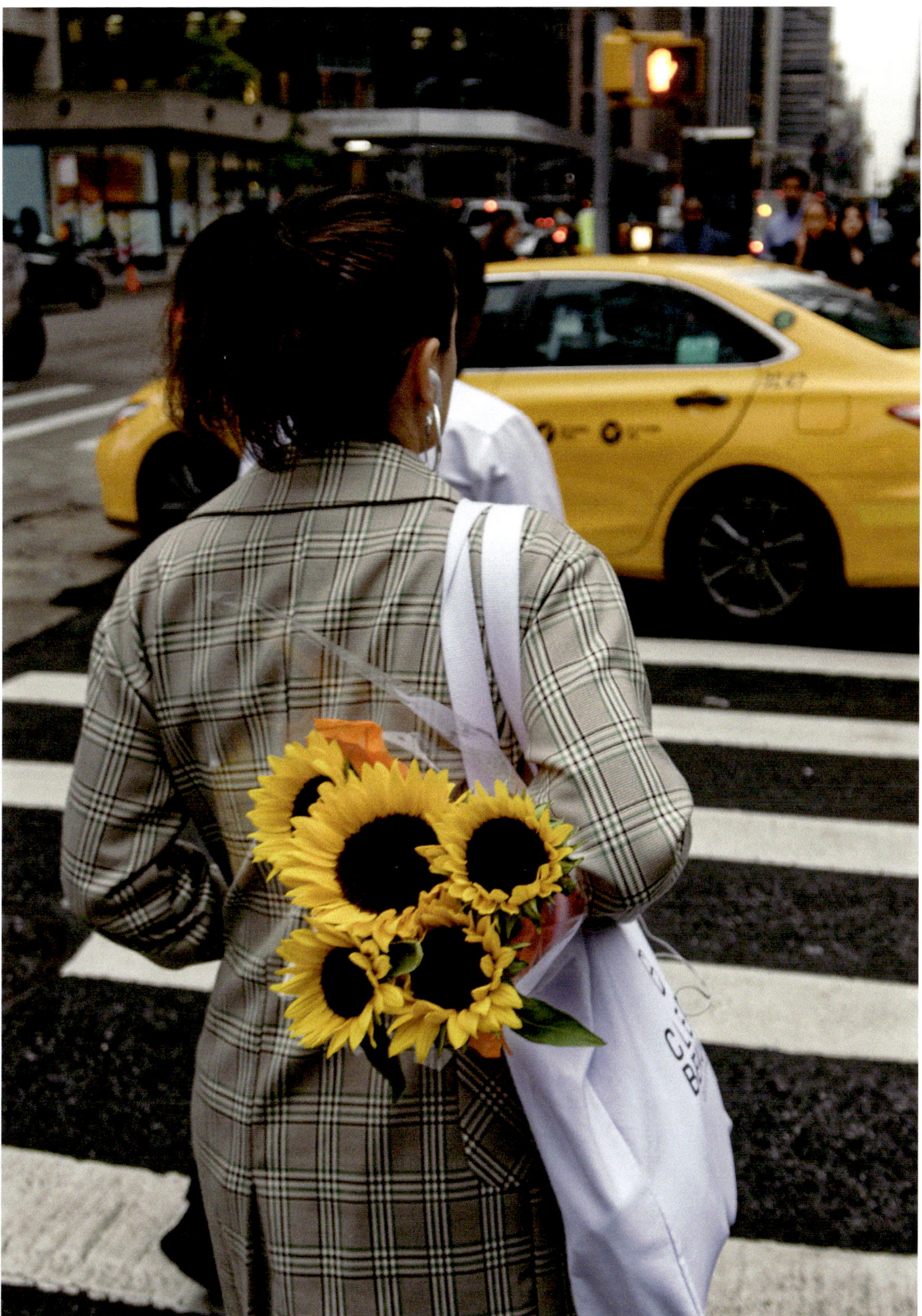

Midtown Manhattan is laid out in a grid pattern, with wide white stripes intersecting the streets to designate crossing areas for pedestrians. After sixty-six years, the culture of jaywalking by impatient New Yorkers was recently legalized. (6th Avenue at West 43rd Street.)

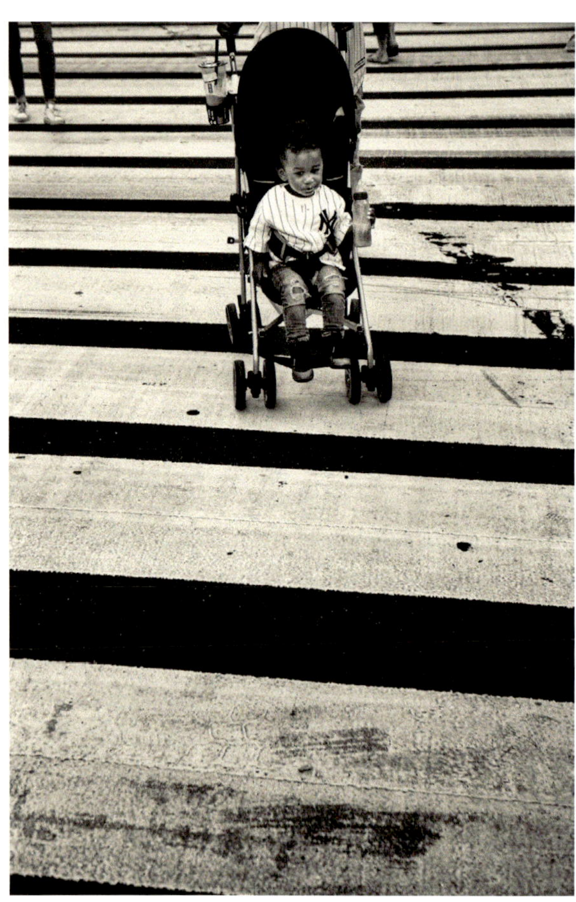

Left: Just as with color, geometric connections materialize. Here, the classic Yankees pinstripes crisscross with the lines of the street. (Broadway at 34th Street.)

Below: In this scene, the "invisible hand" of chance matches up those wearing horizontal stripes with the crosswalk's pattern. (6th Avenue at 32nd Street.)

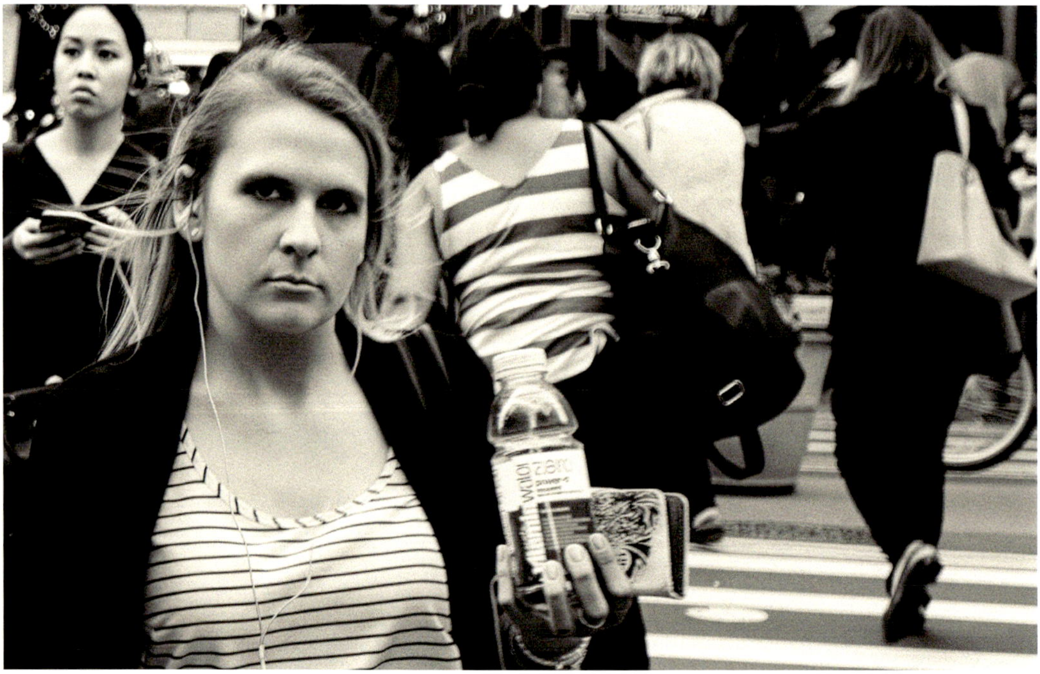

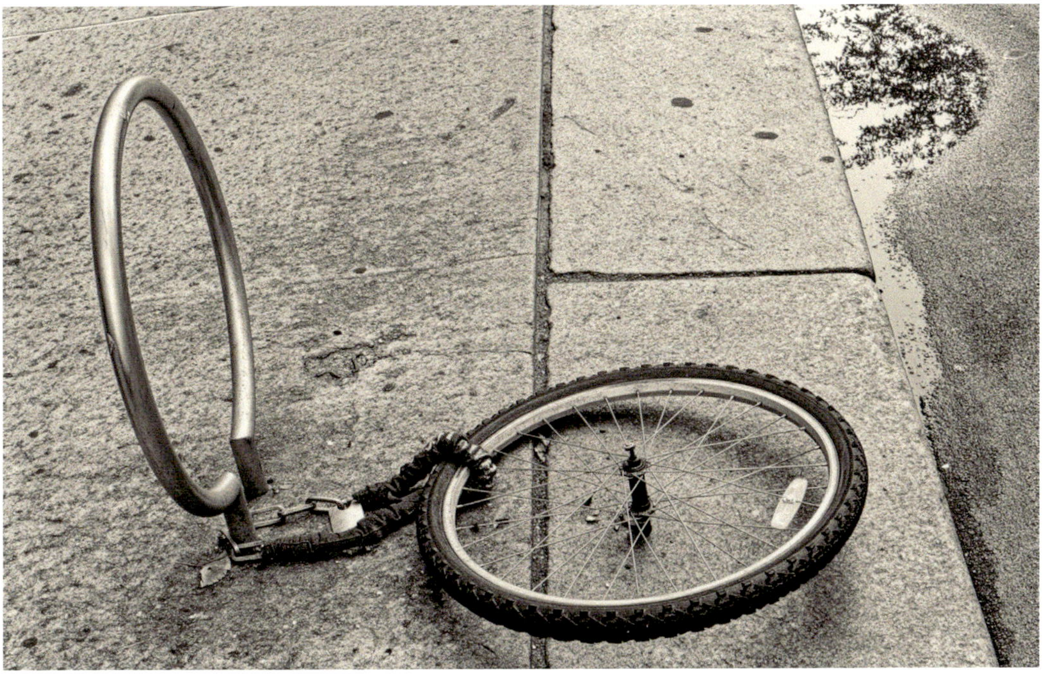

Did someone steal the bicycle and leave the wheel or is it an artistic statement? Whatever the reason, the repeated curves suggest a softness against the right angles and concrete. (Broadway.)

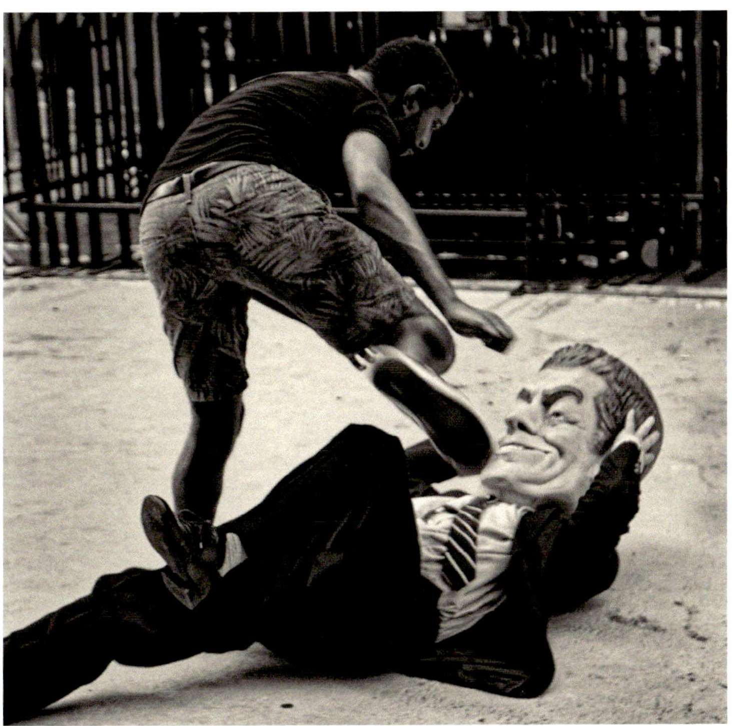

Another mystery is soon confronted. Did they accidentally bump into each other? Is it an assault? Are they engaged in a performance? (Broadway.)

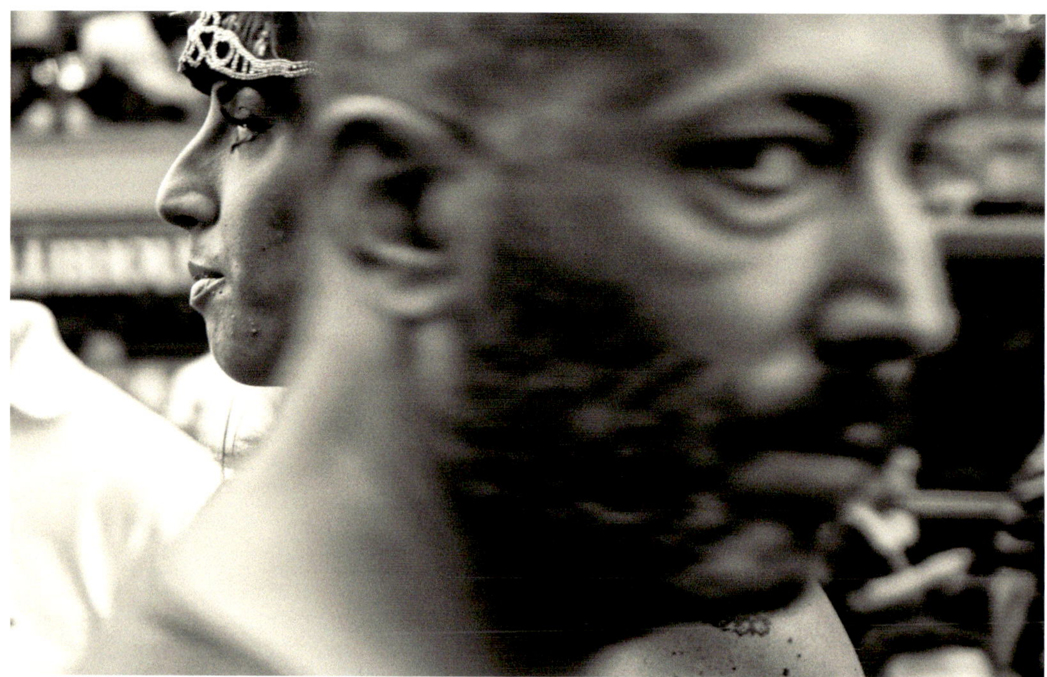

During rush hour, the crowded sidewalks offer a glimpse of other unusual occurrences. (Times Square.)

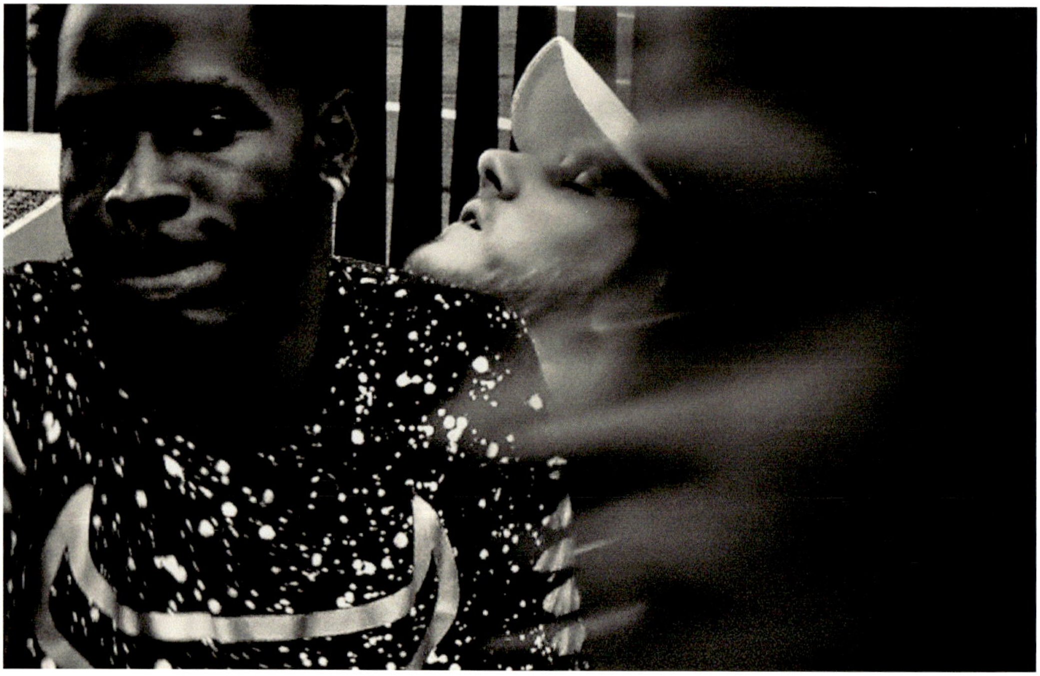

In an instant, a bouquet of heads jumble into a surreal human collage. (Broadway at 42nd Street.)

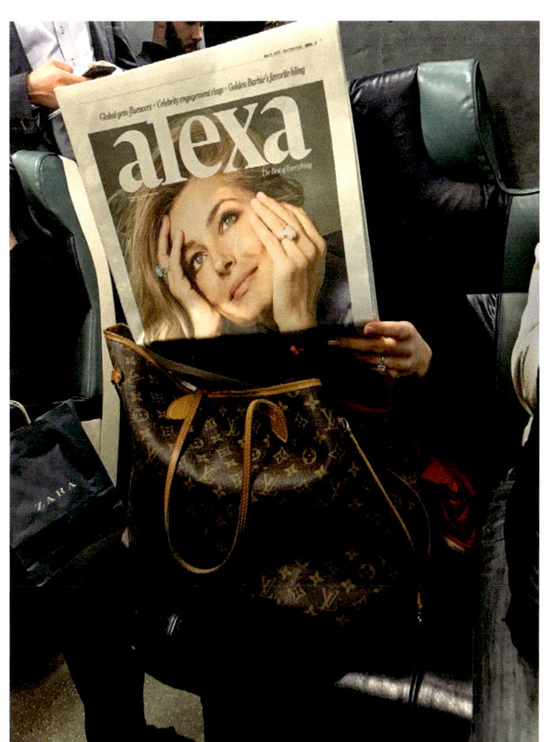

A face may pop up suddenly, like a jack-in-the-box, serving as an impromptu disguise. (Long Island Railroad, Penn Station.)

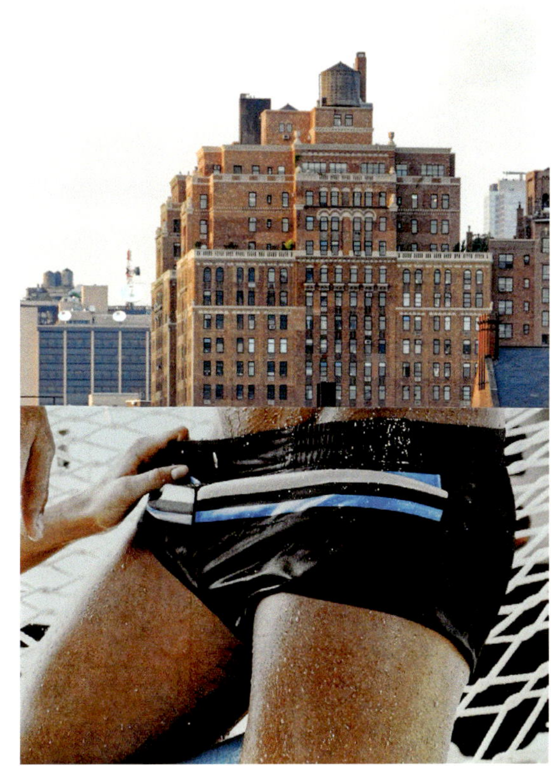

The lower extremities may also make their appearance in the least expected places. (The High Line.)

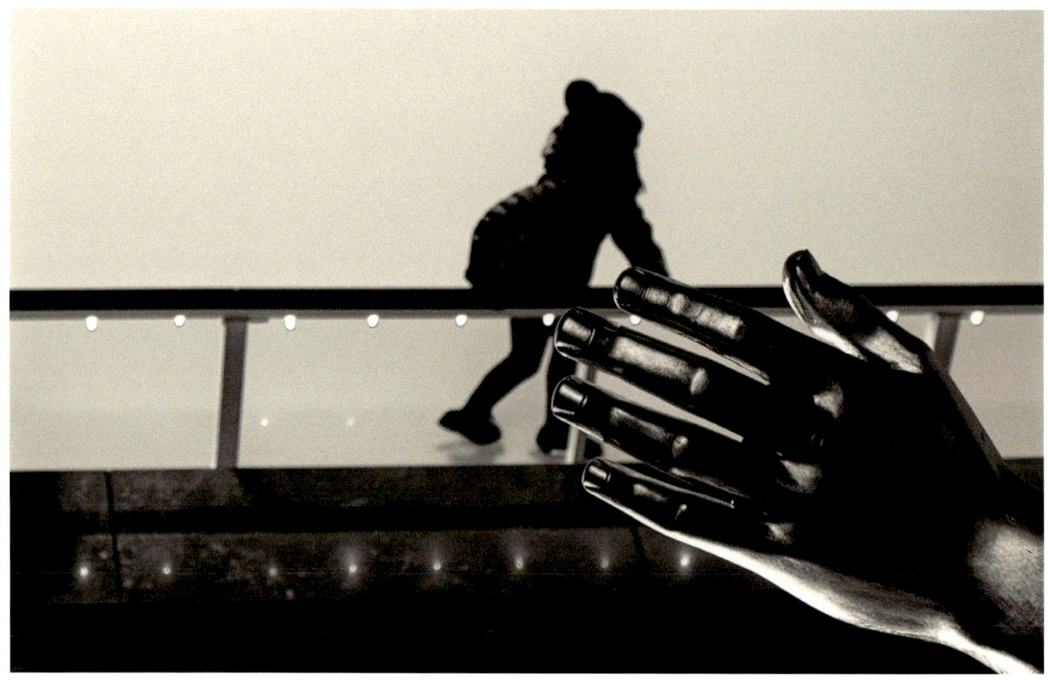

Here, the disembodied hand of the Greek Titan Prometheus seems ready to catch a skater in case she falls. (The Rink at Rockefeller Center.)

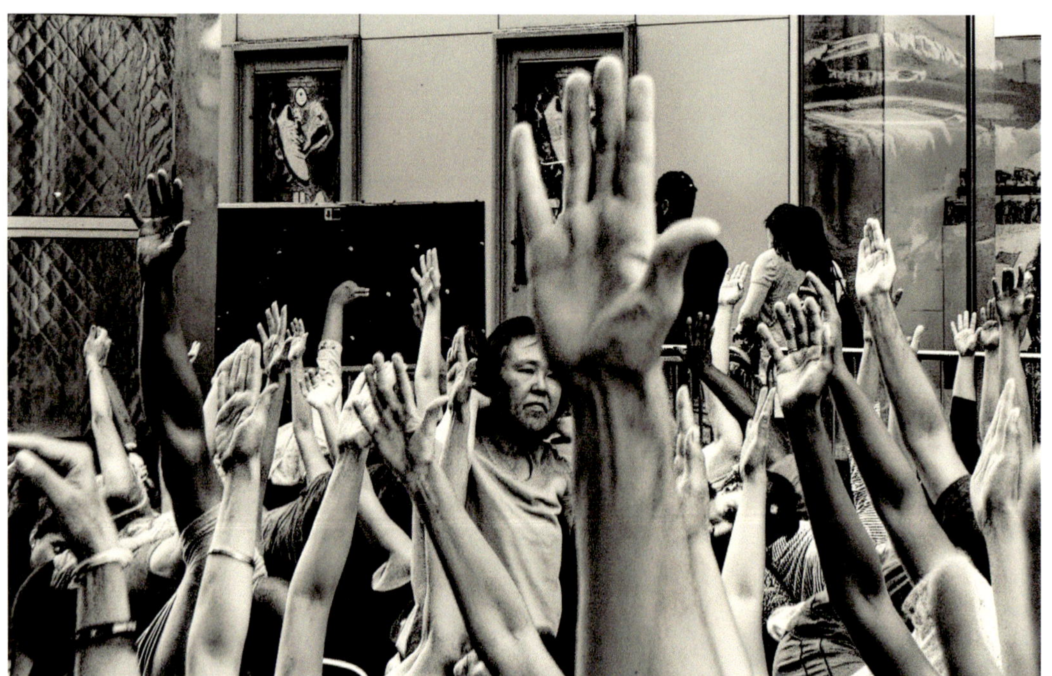

On a different occasion, a couple of blocks away, a woman is surrounded by a forest of outstretched arms. (Times Square.)

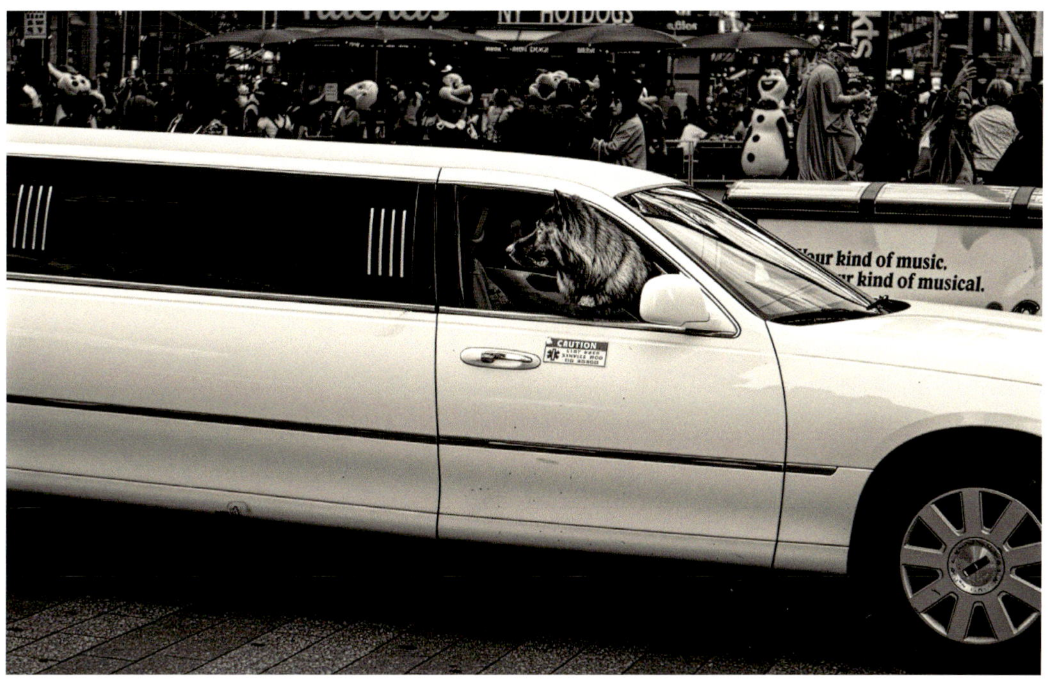

Stretch limousines may not be as popular as they once were in New York, but some special passengers still know how to ride in style. (Times Square.)

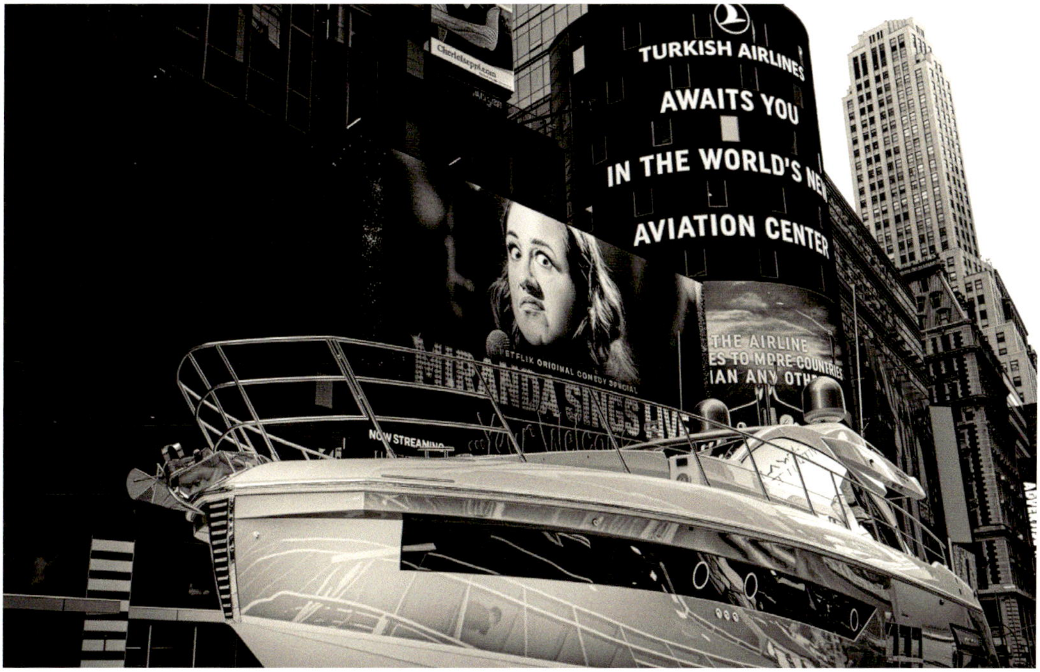

Perhaps a more surprising luxury is the presence of a small yacht in the heart of the city. (Times Square.)

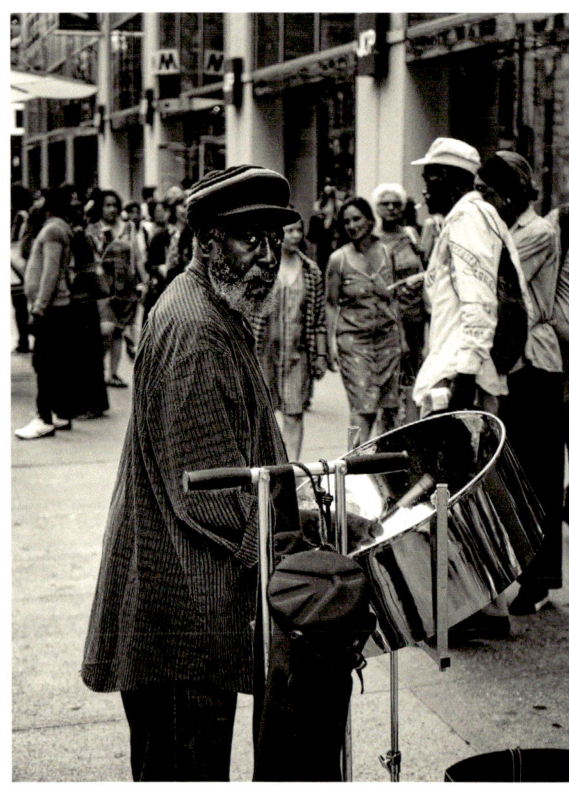

Some folks, like this steel drum musician, do not welcome being startled when approached with a camera. (Broadway at 33rd Street.)

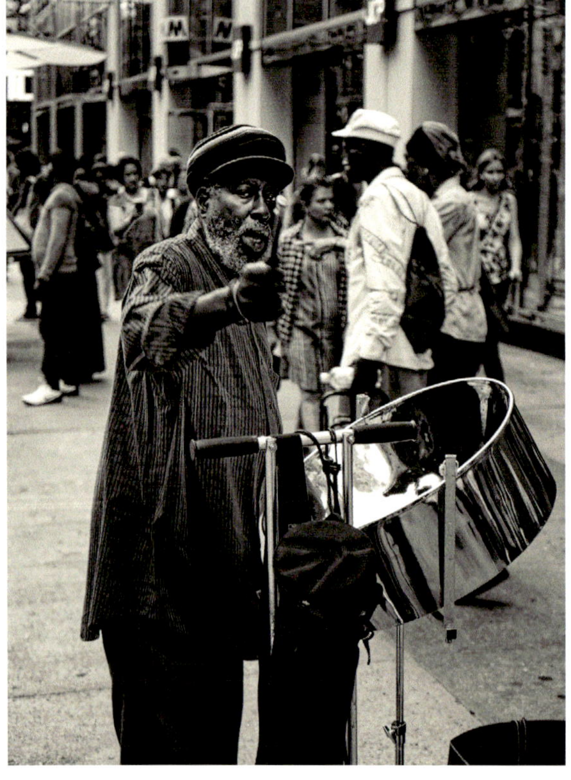

He was upset because someone had recorded a video of his entire performance and uploaded it online. (Broadway at 33rd Street.)

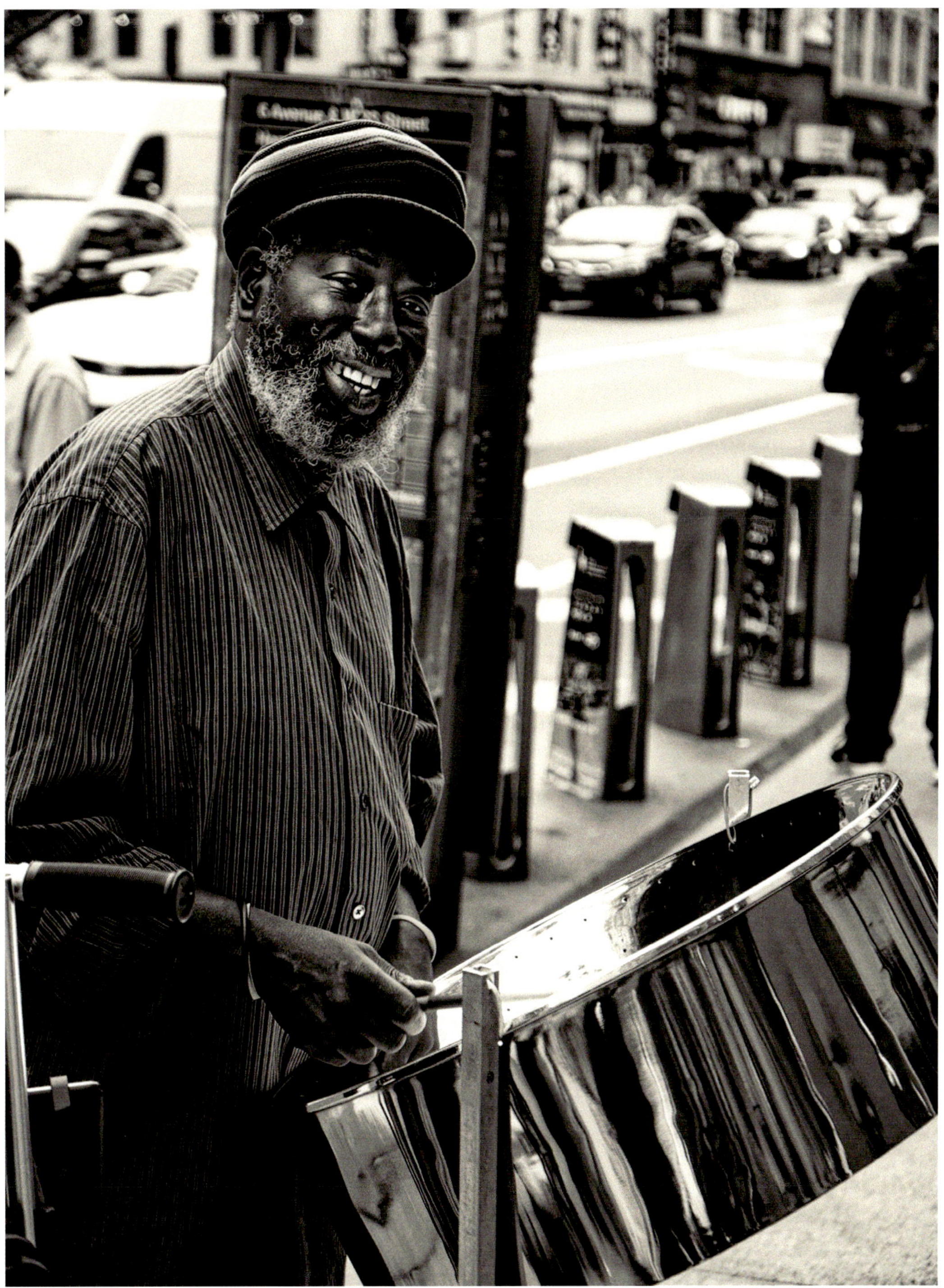

All was forgiven after an apology and an honest explanation of intentions, which elicited a big smile. (Broadway at 33rd Street.)

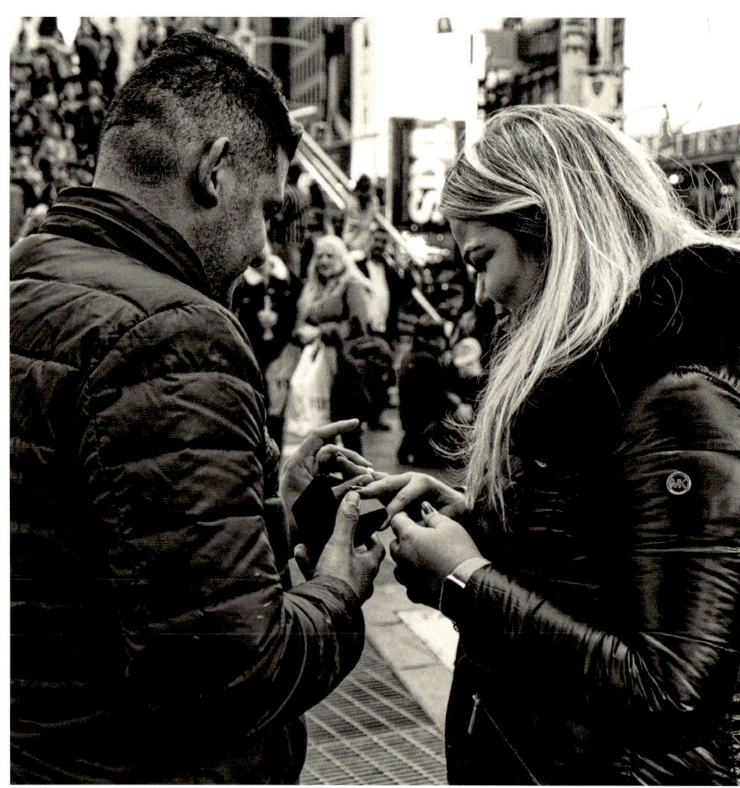

A happier surprise took place at the center of some of the heaviest foot traffic in the city. (Times Square.)

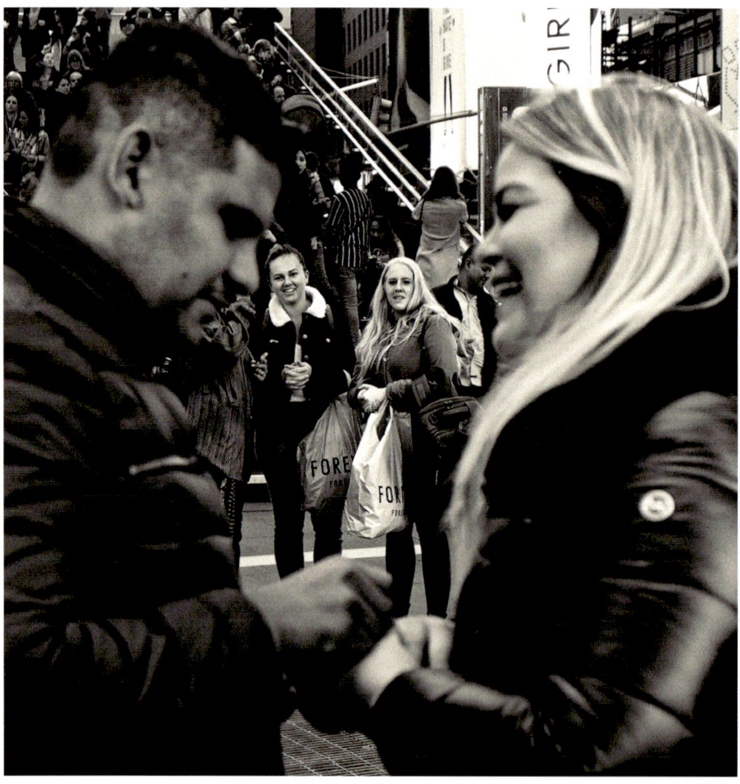

A shared emotional atmosphere arose as shoppers paused, endeared by the unfolding romantic drama. (Times Square.)

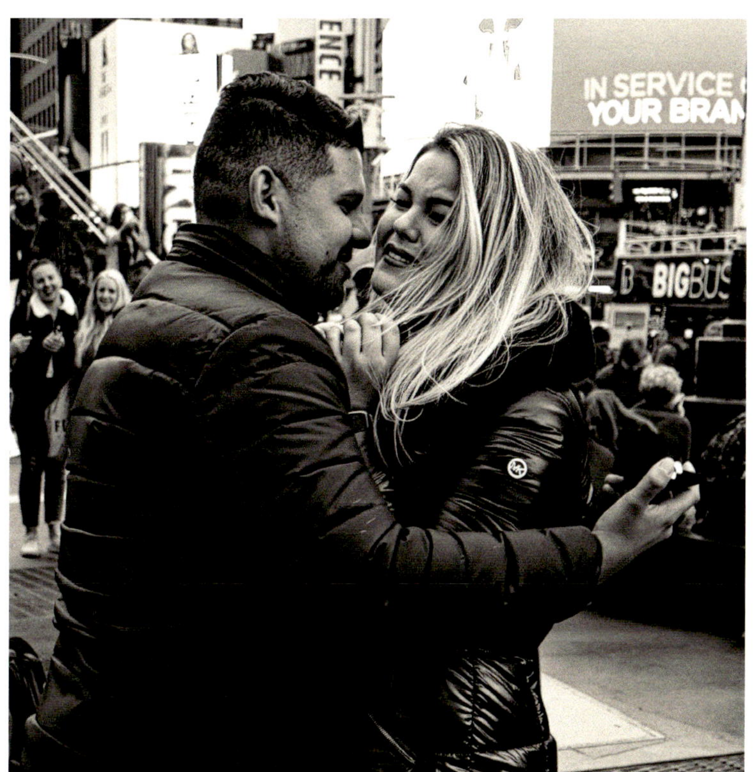

New York may not exude the classic, timeless charm of Paris, but it offers a dynamic, exhilarating setting for Valentine's Day. (Times Square.)

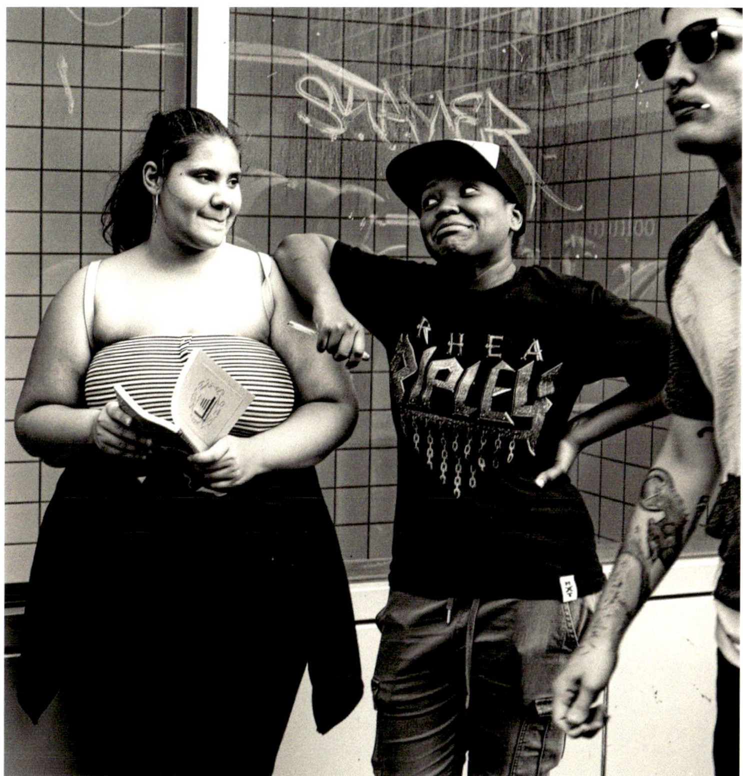

Beyond the city's acclaimed exterior lies an unseen beauty filled with detail, history, color, humor, quirkiness, and split-second coincidences—even in the simple act of daily life. (8th Avenue.)

Afterword

My characterization of New York City is by no means definitive. The Big Apple is always changing and so is my interpretation of it. In a way, the pictures in this book form one giant snapshot unique to the times and locations I experienced. In the years to come, these photographs will likely reveal greater depth and historical significance. What seems ordinary now may become extraordinary with perspective.

Photography and writing are solitary endeavors. Even so, there are many who indirectly contributed to the creation of this book. It began with Sapna Dhandh-Sharma's recommendation of the point-and-shoot camera I purchased. Luke DeLalio, whose artistic opinion I value, encouraged my street photography. Rita Dieguez, Janice Battiste, and Mark Shapiro provided invaluable comments on my manuscript. My thanks to them all. And my thanks to New York City for inspiring and shaping my street photography.

About the Author

The National Park Service commissions Xiomáro to create fine art photographic collections of historical sites, artifacts, and landscapes associated with George Washington, Theodore Roosevelt, and other iconic figures. In between projects, this life-long New Yorker keeps his skills sharp by photographing his encounters in the Big Apple. He was described in a PBS episode as "a historian through the lens" while *The New York Times* described his photographs as having "an unorthodox look" with a "focus on striking details." He is the author of *Weir Farm National Historic Site* (Arcadia Publishing, 2019) with a foreword by Senator Joseph I. Lieberman.

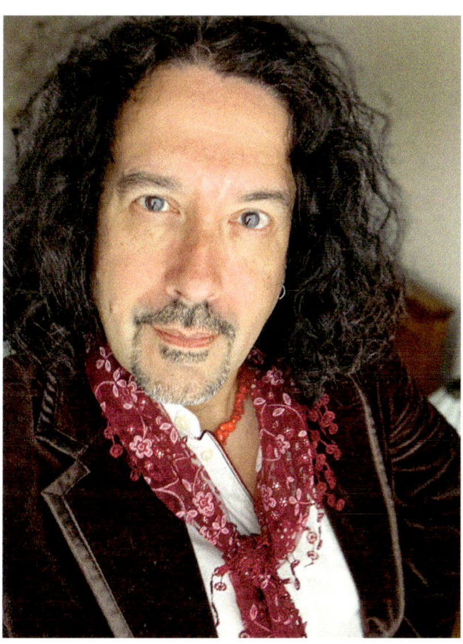

The author, Xiomáro.